Learn my 10 secrets that will help you let go of a broken past and create a life you love.

SINGLE

WOMAN'S

WAKE-UP CALL:

WHY SETTLE FOR LESS
WHEN YOU CAN HAVE MORE

Suntia Smith Publishing
Suntia L. Smith, MSW, LISW-CP

Library of Congress Cataloging-in-Publication Data
Library of Congress Control Number: 2012907177
Author Suntia Smith
Single Woman's Wake Up Call
Why settle for less when you can have more?
ISBN-10: 0985529024
ISBN-13: 978-0985529024

ATTENTION CORPORATIONS, UNIVERSITIES, COLLEGES AND
PROFESSIONAL ORGANIZATIONS: Quantity discounts are available on
bulk purchases of this book for educational, gift purposes, or as premiums
for increasing magazine subscriptions or renewals. Special books or book
excerpts can also be created to fit specific needs. For information, please
contact Suntia Smith Publishing, suntiasmithpublishing@gmail.com
Book Layout ©2013 BookDesignTemplates.com

Dedications

Sometimes in life you meet someone who has the ability to touch the deepest part of your soul and they make such an impact that they leave their hand print. So if they ever go away you keep a part of them tucked inside you. On the good side you have a piece of them with you forever but on the bad side you are always longing for them to come back. And as you grow you begin living a life bigger than yourself, achieving things you never thought was possible. For a long time you wonder what made you so special, why were you able to survive what kept many others hostage. Until one day you look back over your life and see that the hand print was not only on your soul, but on your heart and your future. You then realize your steps were already ordered but you had to make the decision to take the journey.

Now I know the power of love, faith and destiny and I dedicate this book to my love, my faith and my destiny; you will always be remembered.

Contents

NOT A SECRET, JUST A FACT!

My inspiration for writing this book came from conversations with friends, colleagues and other women I have met. It appears that there is a common notion among some single women that it is time to give up on their dreams. Whether it is the dream of having the career they always wanted, finding Mr. Right, or becoming financially stable, the outlook is the same: these women have lost their motivation to make their dreams come true. Due to this lack of motivation, too many single women are settling for "okay" careers, relationships and finances.

Enough is enough, ladies. Okay is not good enough!

As women we deserve better than just being okay. We deserve to live happy, vibrant and successful lives. But we must first stop pretending okay is good enough and realize we have the power to transform our dreams into reality.

Everything you want can be yours if you are motivated to change your life.
You can stop living a life of regrets and shoulda, woulda, couldas. This is your life, and you only have one chance to shine like the star you are!

What to Expect

Before each of my secrets, you will read a never-seen-before blog post and commentary written by me. The blog post was written during times when I was facing the truth about myself, facing hard challenges and changing my life. Each blog post and commentary will give you some insight into the journey of uncovering my secrets and show you how they changed my life. It was hard to share such personal writings, but I wanted to show you that my secrets are not from an overnight success or living a perfect life. My secrets are from real life lessons that have allowed me to stop settling for less than I deserve and start living the life I have always wanted. So, if you are ready to change your life and see all the possibilities awaiting you, continue reading for your official wake-up call.

Blog Post: Where to go from here?

Today I feel stuck, like I am trying so hard and nothing is changing. I give 100% effort and still feel I am at square one. Will I not be successful? Is this all just some type of game I am playing in my mind? I want to be successful. I want to share my dreams and talents with the world, but I don't know. Who motivates the motivator? If I only could just have a glimpse into my future and know it will be worth all of my sacrifice. I am trying to keep smiling, but I feel as though I am the only one who desires change and refuses to settle for just an okay life. I want to scream, I want more, and I want it all. I was created for the life I dreamed of, a life where I am helping other women grow and create successful lives. I want to leave behind something that people can remember me by, something I can be proud of. So I guess I can't give up. I have to keep going, I just have to...

COMMENTARY

I wrote this blog when I was feeling frustrated because I felt alone in my idea of having a better life. I saw so many women giving up their dreams, and it seemed nothing I would say motivated them to see their strengths and possibilities in their future. Here I was, giving it all I had to change my life, and it appeared nothing was happening. Yet despite seeing no change and getting no positive feedback, I decided to keep going. It was as if the dream inside of me would not allow me to give up. So I made up my mind that the best way to motivate women is to live the life I talk about.

And this is where the official wake-up call started: out of frustration, love, and dedication to a better life...
Enjoy!

OFFICIAL WAKE-UP CALL SECRET ONE: LISTEN TO YOUR ALARM OFFICIAL WAKE-UP CALL

To All My Ladies, Time to Get Up and Change Your Life

Have you ever experienced the nagging feeling that something in your life needs to change? If so, you have probably tried to push the feeling away in the hope that it was just a phase. Or maybe you have examined your life and decided everything was okay. Your career, finances and relationships seemed to be going along just fine and you saw no reason to change.

Yet that feeling, which I like to call your inner alarm system, keeps coming back with even more intensity. Your inner alarm system was created to ring when you are off track, in danger or missing something. And maybe now your inner alarm is trying to warn you that you are off track with your goals, in danger of not reaching your full potential and missing the confidence needed to change your life. And if this is true for you, how do you stop your alarm from ringing? How do you begin to change your life?

Well, have you ever heard the phrase, "In order to fix the problem, you first have to admit there is a problem?" This phrase is true with regard to changing our lives.

When we are honest with ourselves, it provides opportunity for us to take a deeper look into the areas of our lives in which we are unhappy. These areas could be your relationships, career or finances, but no matter what challenges you are facing you can change your life. And the first step in changing our lives is transforming our mindset. When our mindset is clogged with negative thoughts, bad experiences, and fear, it blurs our vision of our strengths and abilities. We only focus on our weakness and challenges. Having a negative mindset makes it seem okay to do enough to get by because in your mind, "It doesn't matter anyway." But it does matter because the more complacent you become in your life, the less you believe in yourself. Your confidence decreases and your actions become based on what you can't do versus what you can. When you have low self-confidence, you are more susceptible to settling which is definitely not in our best interest.

Settling is to single women what kryptonite is to superman. Settling makes us weak and confused, breaking down our defenses against the things that suck our strength, such as dead-end jobs, unhealthy re-lationships, family drama, and financial stress. Howev-er, once we renew our mindset to reflect our strengths instead of our weaknesses, we can begin breaking through the barriers that have been holding us back from being successful. Our hopes, dreams, and desires are pushed to the forefront of our minds. With this push, we can roll up our sleeves and do the necessary work to make sure our lives are full of success and happiness.

I want you to know you can do, be and have anything you want when you become committed to changing your life.

Blog post: Blame Game

My mom is gone: the one I loved, the one I wanted to be nothing like, and the one I thought never cared enough. Now that she is gone, whom will I blame? To whom will I say, "It's your fault?"

For the majority of my life, I felt my mom didn't care for me. Now I feel guilty about not caring enough for her, for not seeing her pain or understanding why she could leave me. I want to tell her that no matter how much I ran from her, how much I fought not to be like her, I am so much her daughter. From my laugh to my inner core, I am a lot like her. But it's too late, and I don't understand why other people get a second chance. Other people get to grow into women and make their mothers proud. It is not fair. What do I do with this heartbreak? With my brother's life that I have to mold? What do I have to give to him? Who am I?

COMMENTARY

This blog post was actually a part of a journal entry after my mother passed away. I was overwhelmed with grief and didn't know what direction my life was going. I was concerned for my little brother, who was now solely my responsibility. It was all on me, so if things went wrong, I would have no one to blame but myself. It was time to look in the mirror and see who I was. I had to ask myself some tough questions. It was time I let go of past hurts and started healing so that I could grow into the woman I was destined to be... the woman I am today.

SECRET TWO: FACE THE TRUTH

Mirror, Mirror on the Wall, Help Me Find My Truth Once and for All.

In "Snow White," the evil queen asks the mirror the famous question "Who is the fairest of them all?" And we all know what happened when the mirror told the queen what she didn't want to hear.

But what if I told you that deep down inside herself, the queen already knew Snow White's beauty had surpassed her own? She just didn't want to believe it. The queen would have been happy if the mirror had lied to her so that she could continue living her life in denial. Like the queen, many single women refuse to listen to the voice inside of them that tells them the truth about themselves. But the mirror didn't lie to the queen, and so she had to face what that little voice inside of her had been saying all along: she was no longer the fairest of them all. And although the queen had no control over Snow White's beauty surpassing her own she did have control of how she handled the truth. Instead of embracing the truth and using it to become a better person, she was filled with anger... but why?

Despite the queen's presentation of confidence to others, she was insecure on the inside. And because of her insecurity, the queen thought her only solution was to hide the truth and kill Snow White. But I dare to question what if the queen, after learning the truth, had stepped back and asked herself some important questions such as why she was so obsessed with her beauty. Did she not think she had qualities to offer as queen other than her beauty? What was it about the truth that made her afraid?

Many of us are in relationships, jobs, and family disputes, in which we refuse to face the truth. The truth could be that your relationship is no longer right for you or never was. The truth could be that you are unhappy in your job but are afraid to look into other opportunities. Or maybe the truth is you and your family have different views about the direction of your life, so you must have the courage to walk your own path. But why would we rather continue lying to ourselves than acknowledge the truth and make positive changes in our lives? The reason is that lies allow us to pretend our lives are okay and everything is on the right track; truth reveals areas in our lives that need to change, and that places the responsibility on us.

Facing the truth as to what needs to change in your life requires you to look into your heart and ask some important questions such as:

- Who am I?
- What do I want to achieve in my life?
- What would make me happy?

You may have asked yourself these or similar questions, but because you did not take the time and look inside yourself for the answers, you went for quick answers. Some quick answers could be disguised us unhealthy relationships and foods, excessive material things, insignificant home projects and meaningless sex. However, quick answers are like putting a Band-Aid on a broken arm; it's not going to work, and in many cases it's just going to make things worse because we haven't addressed the real issue. If we are serious about changing our lives, we must stop reaching for quick answers and start confronting past mistakes we've made, bad relationships and disappointments that affect how we feel about ourselves, how we look at the world, and how we pursue our dreams.

Ladies, by holding onto pain from our past, we wake up every day bogged down with all the negativity life has thrown at us. Through my experiences of abandonment, sexual assault, and broken relationships I know very well how negative experiences can make us feel as if we don't have the power to fulfill our dreams. And how not facing painful emotions, whether rejection, disappointment or heartbreak, can lead us to build defense mechanisms to protect ourselves. For example, we might pretend we don't care about specific people, so we don't take chances on love and risk feeling heartbreak again. To this extent, we might do the things everyone else wants us to do so that we will be liked. Whatever defense mechanism you use, it allows you to hide the real you and pretend to be someone else.

Pretending leaves us feeling empty and confused because we can no longer distinguish between what is real and what is fake. As a result, our decisions and action do not reflect what we want or who we want to become, which means we become this person we don't recognize anymore. But we can begin the process of finding ourselves again by facing the truth of where we come from, where we are now, and where we are going. In finding our truth, we confront the pain in our past while discovering how it has affected our actions, thoughts and perceptions. This discovery gives us an opportunity to heal while taking steps to change our lives.

Maybe you have experienced a broken relationship, abuse, financial devastation or loss of a loved one. But whatever your experience was, it has left you doubting yourself, doubting that you could be truly happy again and have the life you desire. I want you to know that painful experiences do not have to define your future;

you can confront those experiences and heal from the pain they caused you.

I remember that for years I buried painful emotions until the day my mother passed away when I was forced to face my truth. I was forced to confront the most painful memory, the one I had always tried to forget. This memory is of me outside playing with my cousins. I heard one of my cousins say, "There goes your momma." When I turned and saw my mother, I ran towards her as fast as I could, thinking this would be the day she would take me home to live with her.

Every time my mother came to visit me at my grand-mother's house, this was what I hoped. This day, my mother kissed me and handed me a bag filled with can-dy. I remember we sat on the steps and then after a few minutes she told me she would be back to see me soon. As soon as I heard the words, "be back," I start-ed to cry and asked why I couldn't go with her. She stood up, and I don't remember exactly what she said, but I know she left me crying. I saw her get into a car and drive away, and oh, how my heart broke. My mother was my first love and also the one who gave me my first heartbreak. Every time she got in her car to leave, I believed she was leaving me because I wasn't good enough. Over and over again, throughout my childhood, I learned to associate love with hurt. I built defense mechanisms such as selfishness, always seeking perfection and not caring for others as a way to not be hurt again.

When my mother passed away I realized that my defense mechanisms did not protect me but stopped me from growing into the woman I was destined to become. I was unable to grow emotionally because I was stuck in the pain I suffered when I was a child. Yes, on the outside I appeared to be okay but on the inside my inner alarm was ringing for me to stop and change my life. The more I grieved for my mother, the more emotions from my past became present in my heart. The memories of all of my mistakes, heartbreaks, and disappointments caused more tears to fall from my eyes. At first I tried to wipe them away, but they began flowing faster so I decided to just let them fall.

As the tears flowed, I started thinking about how I was not the woman I wanted to be. I realized I had been living my life feeling like a motherless child and that I was not good enough to have the life I desired. At that moment, I became this vulnerable person with no defenses, but with just sorrow and tears. I had nothing to do but cry, nowhere to go but on my knees, and no one to call on but God. That was the first time in a long while that I felt I was at the right place.

When I took the first step to start confronting my painful experiences my life began to change. You see the journey of finding our truth causes us to finally be honest with ourselves about those painful experiences that have rocked us to our core. We can acknowledge we have built defense mechanisms to hide the fact that we are broken. This place of honesty provides room in our hearts for forgiveness, forgiveness of our mistakes and forgiveness of people who have hurt us. Forgiveness is a tough part of finding our truth because it can be associated with letting ourselves or someone else off the hook. However, forgiveness is not about excusing the action; it is a process of accepting what happened by acknowledging you cannot change the past.

When we forgive we release the need for any further explanation or obligation from ourselves or others. Forgiving means saying to ourselves, "It was done. I was hurt or I hurt someone else. I acknowledge that it happened. I am sorry that it happened. However, I know I cannot change the past, so I make the decision to accept what happened based on the understanding that I have the power to move forward and have a better life."

When I forgave myself and others I was able to let go my defense mechanisms and stop pretending I was living the life I wanted. I no longer needed protection because I was confident in who I was and where I came from. I became strong enough to let go of people and things in my life that served no purpose. After I let go of the pain that was keeping me stuck, I no longer felt like an imposter in my own body. I could look at my life through new eyes and see what needed to change. It is a great feeling to be free to love myself unconditionally while enjoying all the possibilities life has to offer. Now I am a confident woman who embraces all of herself, the good, bad and ugly. And that is what I desire for you to do in your life. I want you to stop pretending that everything is okay and settling for less than you deserve. I want you to face your truth so that you can begin changing your life in ways you never thought were possible. You are the only one who can take the journey. You are the only one who can create the life you deserve.

Exercise 1: Facing the Truth

I want you to think of your first experience that was the starting point of when you began to doubt yourself and your abilities.

Insight Questions

♠ Who were you with?

_____

_____

♠ What feelings did you experience?

_____

_____

♠ Why do you think you remembered this experience?

_____

_____

♠ What effect did this experience have on how you feel about yourself?

_____

_____

♠ What effect does this experience continue to have on your thoughts, decisions and actions?

_____

_____

Exercise 2: Forgiveness

Forgiveness is the toughest part of finding our truth because it can be associated with letting someone off the hook, whether ourselves or someone else. However, forgiveness is not about excusing the action; it is a process of accepting what happened by acknowledging you have the power to create the life you want.

Insight Questions

♠ Have you forgiven others for the pain they caused you?

_____

_____

♠ If yes, why did you forgive them? If no, why not?

_____

_____

Remember, forgiving means saying to yourself, "It was done. I was hurt or I hurt someone else. I acknowledge that it happened. I am sorry that it happened. However, I know I cannot change the past, so I make the decision to accept what happened based on the understanding that I have the power to move forward and have a better life."

Exercise 3: Letting Go of Defense Mechanisms

Whatever defense mechanism you use, it allows you to hide the real you and pretend to be someone else. You are constantly hiding from your truth in the hope that it will go away. But unfortunately your truth is with you forever, so you must confront it in order to become the woman you are destined to be.

Insight Questions

✦ What defense mechanisms do you use to protect yourself from being hurt again? Examples could be withdrawal, not caring, and conformity.

_____

_____

✦ Why did you choose that defense mechanism?

_____

_____

✦ On a scale of 1 (least vulnerable) to 10 (most vulnerable), identify how vulnerable you would feel without using that defense mechanism?

_____

_____

◢ Are you willing to let go of your defense mechanism?

_____

_____

Exercise 4: Saying it

Once you remember your past, confront it and say goodbye to your defense mechanisms. Now is the time for you to say your truth. After you say it I want you to write it down on an index card.

For example, my index card would read:

My truth is: In my past I have experienced feelings of disappointment, abandonment, and insecurity. Because of my feelings I settled for less than I deserved in my relationships, career, and finances. Today I know the truth that I am strong, beautiful, and loved by others. Because of this truth I no longer need defense mechanisms to protect me. I realize there is nothing from which I need protection. I am not perfect and do not have all the answers. And I remain proud of who I am and need no justification for that.

Once you have written your truth down on an index card, I want you to use it as a bookmark for this book. While reading this book you will be reminded of your truth, so with each secret you discover you will bring your truth along with you. My hope is that by the end of the book you will not need to read your truth anymore because it will become a part of your daily life.

Blog Post: Don't Blush... it's true!

Oh my gosh. I am my worst enemy. I don't see how awesome I am. Today someone gave me a compliment and I tried to debate it. I was told that I was very insightful, and can you believe I tried to talk them out of their compliment? I said, "Not always," and "Sometimes things are very black and white to me." I even said, "I would bet there are more insightful people than me." This person looked at me, smiled and said, "It's okay to accept a compliment."

Hmm, this is true, I thought.

Why couldn't I just say, "Thank you?" I looked back on other instances where I talked myself out of compliments, opportunities and happiness because of my negative thinking. Because I felt so negative about myself, it felt strange for someone to have a positive view of me. Crazy, I know, but true. Something had to change.

I should be the first to give myself a compliment. I should love and appreciate myself. From now on I will say positive things to myself. I will tell myself how insightful, creative, beautiful, and talented I am and I will believe it. I will start to see myself in a positive way. The next time someone gives me a compliment, I will tell them a couple of things they can add...after I tell them how awesome they are!

COMMENTARY

I remember this experience and many like it very clearly. I could never just say thank you to a compliment. I would debate why I didn't deserve the compliment. How crazy is that? But the truth behind the madness is that I didn't believe in the compliments people gave me, so I didn't feel it was the truth.

However, in time, I learned how to become my biggest cheerleader. I know my strengths and challenges and choose to celebrate both because they make me who I am. I look in the mirror and love the woman looking back at me.

See how much I have changed!

SECRET THREE: RENEW YOUR MINDSET

Change from the Inside Out

If you've faced your truth and see that some things in your life need to be different, then you've also seen the woman you wish to become. In order to become the woman you envision, there may be areas in your life you need to change. And even when we want it more than anything, change is hard. When you've done things a certain way your whole life, however negative or unhelpful, those ways become normal and comfortable to you. That's what you know, so you continue those behaviors and think those thoughts, even if they don't produce a positive outcome. Today, we hear the term "dysfunction" spoken so freely that we have forgotten the harm it can do in our lives. Dysfunction is created when we continue to do the same actions expecting a different outcome

However, when you realize, "Hey, my life is not going the way that I want it to go. I'm not where I need to be," the next challenge is doing things differently so that you can move forward.

A renewed mindset is essential in allowing you to let go of negative thoughts and fear which have been holding you back from pursuing your dreams.

How do You Renew Your Mindset?

If you take a step back and listen to your inner voice, you'll realize that you are probably not saying positive things. These negative thoughts are setting you up to fail before you even try to change. It's true! We convince ourselves of all the negative aspects of trying something new and become fearful of the outcome. We tell ourselves, "It won't work anyway," and push aside any possibility of change. In order to feel that our dreams are achievable, we must replace our negative thinking with positive thoughts.

In my first semester of college, I didn't think I belonged there because I was the first one in my family to go to a four-year college and I did not know what to expect from that experience. During the first semester, I didn't know if I would be successful because everyone else seemed to know what they were doing and I felt lost. I definitely had days when I felt like quitting and going home.

I remember I was taking a theology course and everything about this class was difficult, even getting there. It was all the way on the other side of campus, and I always had to run to make it. By the time I got to class, I would be disheveled, scrambling just to be there, let alone understand the lecture. This class required writing and presenting a research paper, and when that assignment came around I was so nervous. I didn't expect to do well at all and my inner voice only reiterated this feeling. I wasn't able to silence those negative thoughts until something incredible happened: I aced the project! From that moment on, I had the confidence that I belonged in college. I knew I could do it. And on my hardest days, I was able to draw on the strength I built by doing well in that one class to keep my inner voice positive and encouraging.

Turn the Negative into a Positive

"I might as well give up."
"Nothing is ever going to change."
"I made that mistake and it's going to haunt me for the rest of my life."
"I have nobody to support me."
"I am not good enough."
"Nobody will ever love me or appreciate me."

These are the types of negative thoughts that can run through our minds all day long. That inner voice can be cruel and hurtful. In order to change those thoughts, first and foremost, you have to believe they are lies. So, the next time you hear that voice inside of you or someone else saying something hurtful, just turn the lie around and tell yourself the truth:

"I don't need to give up. I need to keep going until I get it."
"I have the power to make change in my life."
"My mistakes are in the past and they don't control my future."
"Every day is a new day."
"I deserve the best."
"I love me."

Doesn't that sound better? Doesn't it feel better?

I am a great believer in writing and saying positive self-affirmations everyday so that they become part of your belief system. You may have times when you feel down on yourself but when you have positive affirmations available you can lift yourself back up and find the strength to make positive changes in your behavior.

When it comes to changing your behavior you have to start looking for ways to make your dreams come true. If you want a certain type of job, then find out what education and skills you'll need. If you want to save money to buy a house, think about how you can change your budget and spending habits. That's when you start stepping outside of your comfort zone to make changes, develop new habits and move toward your goal.

It may be difficult but if it's something that you really want and you see how it will benefit you, then take one step at a time to accomplish your goal. You always have the choice of whether to stay where you are or do what it takes to move forward. Once you make the choice to move forward your possibilities will be endless.

Surround Yourself with Positive People

Surrounding yourself with positive people is an effective way to make sure your renewed mindset remains focused on your future. Positive people will build you up, encourage you, and offer to help when they see you are in need. However, some people are always negative, forever complaining and trying to bring everyone around them down. They may not be doing it intentionally but negativity is all they know.

When your own mindset is negative, it can be difficult to tell who has your best interest in mind because negativity will seem normal to you. But once you make the decision to revive your dreams and start getting rid of your own negative thinking, you'll see other peoples' negativity clearly. Usually, when you share your dreams with negative people they'll say something to shoot you down. For example, if you say you're thinking about going back to school or you're trying to save money to buy a house, they'll sneer, "That's a bad idea," or "You're not going to have time for that," or "I wouldn't do that if I were you." Negative people will not support your goals because they are not able to see the possibility of success for themselves. Therefore, when you hear negative comments, find the strength to take a deep breath and know it's not you – it's them.

As soon as you realize someone in your life doesn't want you to do better for yourself, you must distance yourself from them. This can be difficult, especially in the case when the negative person is a family member however in such situations you can establish boundaries.

Remember, the only person who has to believe in your dream is you. Once you realize that, then you will find the courage to stay on the right path to change your life. Do not allow anyone to distract you from reaching your goals. You may have to allow some calls to go to voicemail, miss some events or go home early some nights, but these are small sacrifices you will have to make in order to create the life you desire. Become passionate about changing your life and seize every positive opportunity that will get you a step closer.

Whether it is going back to school, starting a new career or buying your first home, it can be challenging to meet new people in different environments. But we all need to step outside of our comfort zones in order to grow. The new people you meet could become a part of your support system and encourage you to pursue your goals. Although you may not realize it at first, these people can support you the best because they are traveling their own unique journey. Writing this book has been a long-time dream of mine, but it hasn't been easy. If I hit a wall, had writer's block, felt as if things weren't going the way I expected, or just got scared, I had certain friends who I knew I could call when I needed them. I have surrounded myself with positive people and they play an important role in my life.

I have one friend who is the loudest cheerleader. If I call her, she supports me, encourages me and expresses strong belief in my ability.

After I talk to her, I feel great. I feel as if I can do anything. If I can't reach her, I have another friend I can call. Each friend has a different personality and they encourage me in different ways. When I get off the phone with any of them, I feel better. I feel I can achieve my dreams.

That's why it's vital to have those positive people in your life because they see you for who you really are. They see your strength and purpose. These friends give you the confidence to dust yourself off and say, "I had a bad day, but I am still capable of achieving my goals."

As you start surrounding yourself with positive people, distancing yourself from those who don't support you, and stepping outside your comfort zone, you will become stronger. This will be a boost of self-esteem because positive actions give you power. You can take control of your life. When you see yourself achieving those victories, even the small ones, you'll see more possibilities for yourself, including the possibility that the life you dreamed of is in your reach. Be open to all the people you can help, and all the goals you can accomplish. When you do, doors you never knew existed are going to start opening up for you because you're more confident and refuse to settle for less than you deserve. Even when you get tired, keep going until the life you imagine, is the life you have.

Exercise 5: Change from the Inside Out

Now it is time you begin changing your negative thoughts into positive ones. Our daily thoughts play a major role in how we feel about ourselves and our confidence. When we start having positive thoughts we start believing in our abilities and strengths.

On an index card I want you to write 3 negative thoughts/statements you have said to yourself or someone has said about you. On the opposite side of the index card I want you to write 3 positive statements that will change the negativity in your mind.

After you have finished, turn the card so that only positive thoughts are facing up. I would like for you to put these cards in items that you take with you everywhere, such as a planner, purse, or workbag. Each day, whether you have a negative thought or not, I want you to read a positive thought from your cards. Read the positive thoughts each day until you are thinking them automatically!

For example:

- I might as well give up vs. I have the power to make change in my life
- No one will ever love me vs. I am worthy of love
- No one will ever forgive me vs. Every day is a new day

Exercise 6: Surrounding Yourself with Positive People

Remaining positive is something we must work at daily because we live in a society where everyone will not share our viewpoints. We must be able to recognize when sharing our dreams with certain people affects us negatively.

In this exercise, I want you to think about experiences when you have shared your dreams with people and the feeling and responses you received from them were positive or negative. Then I want you to review the criteria below to categorize the negative and positive people in your life.

Some criteria for determining the positive people in your life are:

◢ They are supportive of you and your dreams.

_____

_____

◢ They offer assistance and resources when you are in need.

_____

_____

◢ They say encouraging words when you are feeling down or overwhelmed.

_____

_____

🔺 They provide a viewpoint that allows you to see your challenges and strengths.

_____

_____

Some criteria to determine the negative people in your life:

🔺 They only provide you with the reason why you "can't" do something.

_____

_____

🔺 They remind you of past mistakes or bad experiences to make you feel inadequate to achieving your dreams.

_____

_____

🔺 They constantly provide negative comments about you, themselves, and others.

_____

_____

◢ They are in a position to help you but do not offer assistance.

_____

_____

With regard to the people you find to be positive in your life, I want you to write down ideas of how you can spend more time with them. For example, you might invite them to lunch or dinner, add an extra phone call to them during the week, or plan an event that you both can attend. Remember, spending more time with positive people will encourage you to be your best and not settle for less than what you deserve.

Now, with regard to the people you find to be negative in your life, I want you to write down ideas of how you can spend less time with them. For example, you might limit the information you share with them about your goals and challenges and cease to engage in negative conversations about yourself or others.

Not a Secret, Just a Fact

Good Decisions Are a Girl's Best Friend

So how do we start making good decisions? We start by owning our power and accepting the responsibility for changing our lives. We must realize that good decision making is not magic. We can't say "Abrakazam" and realize the right thing to do. Many of us have actually tried the magic method, hoping our decisions are right and that everything will turn out fine. But we have to stop hoping and start thinking through how each potential decision will affect our lives. Yes, some decisions will be difficult and require sacrifices. But what is life without sacrifice? If you are not willing to sacrifice for your own future, then who will? If you keep making the same bad decisions, you will keep getting the same outcomes.

The art of making good decisions is taking time to see in what ways that decision will affect your life. When you are contemplating a decision you should ask yourself one important question: how will this decision affect my life tomorrow, in six months and in one year? Asking yourself this question allows you to look past the moment and see the effect your decision will have on your future. Yes, we should be excited about our decisions but we don't want that excitement to overshadow our thought process. Remember, anything worth having is worth sacrificing for.

For example, if you want to buy a new home, you may have to sacrifice taking some vacations or going shopping as often as you like, but just think about walking into your new home knowing it's yours. You ladies who want to start a new career or advance in your current one, you will have to sacrifice your time. You may have to go back to school, attend workshops, or participate in new activities. But look ahead and imagine that you get the new job or promotion. All of those late-nights studying and practicing will bring you the reward of success. These moments are priceless! During those moments you realize that all your hard work was worth it.

Ladies, we are the CEOs of our lives, and in order to stay at the top of our game we must make good decisions. The problem is that decision-making isn't easy, and some women subconsciously avoid it. You may have had experiences in your past that lead you to believe the outcome is going to be negative no matter what you do. However, if we want different outcomes, we must start with different attitudes and behaviors.

Making the kinds of changes in your life that we've been talking about is not easy work. You may have questions in your mind: Can I do this? Is it really worth it? Is this for me? Along with these questions, you may feel fear. But I want you to think past the fear and focus on the future you desire. If you truly want to change, my answers to your questions are: Yes, this information is for you. Yes, changing your life will be worth it. Yes, you can really have the life you desire. You have started on this journey of finding out who you are, what you want and how to get it, so why stop now?

Answer the following questions before moving to the next chapter.

- ✦ Will you start taking the time to make better decisions?
- ✦ Will you stop allowing other people's opinions to dictate your decisions?
- ✦ Will you make your dreams a priority?

I hope your answer is a yes because you are too smart and fabulous to settle for less than what you deserve.

Blog Post: What About Me?

Today was one of those days when I wanted to go home and start over. Nothing was going right. I forgot my morning snack, Jamal was complaining about school, I had writer's block the night before and to top it all off, I received an email stating I was scheduled for a late meeting, so I won't make my exercise class.

What is a girl to do? I need something, or I am going to scream. I feel so out of whack. Why am I so angry? Well, I guess anger is not what I am feeling. I am frustrated. Frustrated that I am trying to do everything for everybody and I am not taking care of myself. Frustrated I can't be one of those women in the PTA who visit their children's school regularly. Frustrated that my business is not where I want it to be.

Things have to get better. I can't let things build up like this. I have to do something.

COMMENTARY

When I wrote this I was trying to be everything to everyone and was left feeling exhausted and frustrated. I realized if I continued to neglect myself I wouldn't be able to do anything. So I decided to fight the guilty feeling of spending time alone. I went into a quiet place and refused to be interrupted. I just thought about my day and things I wanted to accomplish. That first night I slept great and woke up refreshed, so I decided to continue taking time for myself. Now it is a part of my nightly routine.

SECRET FOUR: SELF-REFLECTION

Beauty Is in the Eye of the Beholder

You may have lost yourself like I did by trying to be everything to everyone. So, how do we make sure we never lose ourselves again? And, most importantly, how do we hold on to our truth? The answer is self-reflection. For many of us, New Year's is the only time when we take a look at our lives and decide what stays, what goes, and what needs to change. We make goals, such as losing weight, changing jobs, going back to school or making our relationships better, but some-where along the way we usually lose our motivation. Work, family, and daily stress take the focus away from our goals and place it on our problems. Before you know it, another year has passed, and you're still stuck in the same place.

Our goals, even the ones we make with the best intentions, get away from us. Why? Because if we're not taking time to check in with our goals, we forget them. Nightly self-reflection is the most effective tool that has helped me stay in touch with who I am, my goals and my future.

Self-reflection during the day is fine, but it's different from nightly self-reflection in a couple of ways. When you reflect during the day, you are usually in the middle of doing something. You may be in the car driving to a destination, in the shower getting ready to go somewhere, or having a quick break before your next appointment. In nightly self-reflection, you take yourself out of the hectic day and focus only on you. You cannot do this driving because you have to pay attention to the road and other drivers. You cannot do this while taking a shower or between appointments because at those times you're already thinking about the next thing on your schedule.

In nightly self-reflection, there are to be no cell phones, televisions, family, lovers, or friends. You are the focus and center of your attention. Scheduling this for the same time each night will help you to get in the routine of self-reflection. However, the time may change, depending on your schedule.

Each night I use the following steps to reflect on my daily actions, thoughts and words.

Step one of self-reflection is matching your experiences with your emotions.

During your nightly self-reflection there should be silence. The next day's schedules or responsibilities should not be on your mind. Once you are in your quiet place, I want you to think about your day and the experiences you encountered. This may bring up some emotions. Some emotions may feel good and some may not feel so good, but I want you to give yourself permission to feel all of them. Once you feel them, I want you to think about why each experience made you feel that particular emotion.

Step two of self-reflection is honesty.

To be effective in our lives we must learn how to be honest with ourselves. During self-reflection our thoughts and emotions are the only things that matter. We don't have to worry about how it will make someone else feel, so we can feel safe to start answering the question of why certain experiences would make us feel different emotions. Going one step further, we discover where those emotions come from. This isn't always easy. But in the self-reflection process, I learned honesty is an essential part of better understanding ourselves and our emotions. Understanding our emotions helps bring clarity to our actions because our actions reflect our emotions. In many cases, when we get angry with someone, leave a job, get into a relationship, or make some other big decision, it is all based on unacknowledged emotions.

Step three of self-reflection is to make peace with your day.
Making peace with your day is accepting any mistakes you may have made, whether in your actions, or words. For self-reflection to be effective, you must forgive yourself nightly. And the key to forgiving yourself nightly is to understand you did the best you could today and tomorrow you have the power to do better. With this understanding, you can start eliminating any negative mental and emotional baggage from your life.

I know forgiving yourself everyday may seem an extreme step, but it allows you to begin the next day afresh. You will no longer take the worry of one day into another, which leads to a more stress-free and confident you. Once you have made peace with your day, it is time to rest. Do not return telephone calls, begin working on a project, or watch a television show. These new activities can cause new emotions to come up that may have a negative effect on your sleep and into the next day.

The Purpose of Self-Reflection

This powerful self-reflection process allows me to connect with myself each day so that I become aware of the things that are stressing me or progressing me in my life.

You will gain a clear picture of what is holding you back from achieving your goals, whether it is personal, professional, or financial. With that clear picture, you can make daily changes to stay on track and never lose yourself again. Remember, your truth includes your past, present, and future, so you need tools in place to make sure one aspect of your life is not negatively affecting the other.

Regularly practicing nightly self-reflection keeps our goals right in front of us. It allows us to acknowledge progress and challenges in achieving our goals. Through self-reflection we can be honest about our progress and make necessary adjustments to move forward. I go through the self-reflection process at the end of every day by sitting in a quiet place and writing in my journal. I revisit all the day's experiences that affected me either negatively or positively and consider my responses and feelings in each situation. At least once a month I take even more self-reflection time and check in with my short- and long-term goals: whether or not I'm getting closer to them, where I need to change my course, what obstacles I faced over the previous weeks, and what I learned along the way. You can write in your journal during your self-reflection time or just sit quietly and think. I prefer to use my journal because it allows me to write my thoughts and feelings about different experiences and look at them later. I love looking back in my journal and seeing my personal growth and progress towards my goals. A journal provides a record of challenges and accomplishments in life, so we can remember how far we have come.

Whatever method you use, daily and monthly self-reflection time will help you greatly in reaching your goals. I know life is hectic and you don't need one more thing on your to-do list, but you are worth making time for yourself.

And speaking of time for you, nightly self-reflection is a great way to do just that! In our busy lives, we are constantly interacting with people, whether on the phone, face-to-face, or on the Internet.

It seems we have to make an appointment with ourselves just to be alone. As women, we have a tendency to nurture everyone else and leave our needs and wants on the back burner. We lose sight of our goals and what would make us happy because we are so busy helping everyone else. We must instead have balance between helping the ones we love and helping ourselves. Balance starts with taking time alone each day to self-reflect on our progress and our challenges.

During self-reflection we make sure we are not ignoring red flags or building defense mechanisms, all the old behaviors that didn't serve us well. I know everyone depends on us, but if we don't take care of ourselves then we won't have anything to give others. When we try to give to others when running on empty, we lose balance and become stressed and overwhelmed. During this off-balance state, our minds become vulnerable to negative thoughts and confusion because we are not mentally strong enough to fight them.

Nightly check-in helps strengthen us by giving us alone time. Don't worry, taking time for yourself does not mean that you are selfish, but that you value who you are. When you value who you are, you take care of yourself. And that is exactly what we do with nightly self-reflection: we take care of us.

Exercise 7: Self-Reflection

Self-reflection has become a major part of my process of changing my life, and I want to show you how it can help you change yours. Tonight, I want you to review this chapter and follow the steps provided to reflect on your actions, thoughts, and words for today.

◎   Match your experiences with your emotions.

_____

_____

_____

◎   Be honest with yourself.

_____

_____

_____

◎   Make peace with your day.

_____

_____

_____

Blog Post: Never Knew What You Meant to Me

Today I spoke with my father for the first time in four years. Our relationship has always been on-and-off-again since I was a little girl. I met my father for the first time that I can remember when I was ten years old, and I was so amazed by him. I would watch him carefully to see if our nose or eyes were the same. I listened to his every word waiting for him to call my name, waiting to do a dance or tell him what I did in school so that he would be proud of me. I always wanted to be a daddy's girl. It is something about having a father who loves you in your life that brings happiness and confidence into the soul of a little girl. And when you don't have a father in your life, a void is left.

COMMENTARY

I spent most of my life trying to fill that void of not having my father in my life. I was looking for a love that would always be there, an unconditional love. I would never have admitted it before, but I needed the love only a father could give. Thankfully, I found love in God who has showered me with His love. And just when I thought God had spoiled me enough, He gave me another blessing: my father called me. All the anger, all the questions, and all the bitterness went away when I heard his voice. It was as if God filled my cup with His love, and now He was making it overflow by bringing my father back into my life.

Secret Five: Growing Close to an Unconditional Love

You Are Loved Regardless

Growing up as little girls, most of us yearned for attention from our fathers. We wanted to hear them say "That's Daddy's little girl," or, "I am proud of you." And most of all we wanted to hear him say, "I love you." If you had a father who said these loving words, it may be hard to picture growing up without your father's support. But for some women, including myself, this is a reality. We grew up imagining that one day our father would say he was sorry for not being there for us. He would take us in his arms and make us feel like princesses. Our fathers would finally make us feel loved and beautiful.

However, when we became older, our imagination was no longer able to fill the void left in our lives by our fathers. So, we went in search of a love that would make us feel beautiful. Some of us purchased unnecessary material things, some entered into unhealthy relationships, and some settled into the "safe zone" because we were scared of being hurt. Some of us put on our Ms. Perfect attitude, pretending everything was okay. But whatever actions we took to make the hurt from our absent fathers go away was just a distraction from the void and in many cases brought more pain into our lives.

At times I would enter into relationships hoping to find this love I had been yearning for all my life. I wanted a love I could trust and depend on to be there always. But I realized that my quest to fill the void my father left blinded me both to warnings to get out of a relationship and to any positive signs that a man truly loved me. In actuality I was looking for a man to love me in the same way my father should have, and that was impossible for a man to do. The only means to replace a fatherless void in your life is receiving unconditional love from a power greater than you. For me, that power was God. In college, I experienced God's unconditional love when I needed it the most. I was assaulted and threatened to have my life taken by someone I mistakenly thought loved me because I was so broken on the inside.

During that tragic time so many thoughts were going through my head. I had no idea if I were going to live or die, but I thought back to the time when I was a little girl and my grandmother told me, "Whenever you are in trouble, pray and call on the name of Jesus." And that was what I did. Over and over in my mind, I prayed and called on the name of Jesus. And I am here today to tell you that whatever father you did or didn't have, whoever didn't love you or make you feel beautiful, you were created with a divine purpose. And because of that purpose and love, you no longer have to run after love or cry for it because we know we have the greatest love of all. I didn't understand why I was saved from being killed that night. I was a girl who thought she knew everything and needed nobody. Now, I am grateful that God's love is not based upon what I do or how I see Him but on who He is and who He says I am. Once I realized there was nothing I could do to separate me from God's unconditional love, the void left by my father was filled.

I now understand that perfection is unobtainable and God's love is undeniable.

Ladies, we must look into our hearts and confront those voids that are causing us to continue to make mistakes we cannot afford. These voids are stopping us from seeing the truth of who we are and what we can become. Let's not waste any more time by living a life without purpose and passion. You're starting every morning by wanting to go back to sleep because your life has become something you dread. Not having it all together should not stop you from opening your heart to an unconditional love in which you can trust. No more insecurity and trying to fill voids from your past with negative behaviors and superficial living. You can walk with your head up high knowing you are connected to a love that is greater than you. Feeling loved unconditionally will provide you a boost of confidence; confidence that can lead you to a new and exciting journey in life.

Exercise 8: Growing Close to an Unconditional Love

Being loved unconditionally is a wonderful feeling and builds confidence within ourselves so that we no longer seek out things and relationships that are not good for us. Below are questions I want you to answer to give you more insight into unconditional love and how it affects your life.

⊙ What voids do you feel in your life?

_____
_____
_____
_____

⊙ What things and/or relationships have you used to try and fill your voids?

_____
_____
_____
_____

⊙ Have you ever felt unconditional love? If so from whom?

_____
_____
_____
_____

◎ If you have ever felt unconditional love, how has it affected your life?

_____
_____
_____
_____

◎ Do you have a source of power greater than yourself that you believe in?

_____
_____
_____
_____

◎ Do you think continually receiving unconditional love would change your life?

_____
_____
_____
_____

Not a Secret: Just a Fact
You Are Beautiful

When I wait in line at the grocery store, I see images of women with designer clothes, beautiful hair, and flawless skin plastered on the covers of magazines. When I turn on the television, each woman looks almost the same as the last: a cookie-cutter image of something society tells us represents beauty.

I know we've all heard that looks matter, being beautiful is important, and that if we don't look a certain way, we might as well forget it. Some of us have bought into the idea that there is something missing from our lives that will make us beautiful. So we run out and buy the latest makeup, clothes, and accessories.

However, by the time you have read what the hottest trend is this month someone else is already writing what the hottest trend will be for next month. This creates a never-ending cycle of feeling that you are not good enough.

I want you to break that cycle and know you are beautiful because of who you are and not what you look like. Let's face it: with the right makeup, hair, clothes, and plastic surgeon, anyone today can become beautiful on the outside. Our society puts so much emphasis on being the perfect beauty that women skip steps such as improving self-esteem, attitude, and actions and jump right into working on their appearance.

The result is the creation of insecure women who depend on their looks and possessions to make them feel valuable, but what they fail to realize is that beauty radiates from the inside-out. If we put the same focus (or more) on becoming beautiful on the inside as we do on being beautiful on the outside, we will forever radiate beauty and love in everything we do.

We must stop trying to become this perfect woman we see on television and in magazines. These women have been through wardrobe, hair, and makeup sessions. Their magazine images have been airbrushed and edited to delete blemishes. So why do we continue to beat ourselves up when we can't achieve their look? It's because we don't believe we are beautiful just the way we are.

We have it in our minds that beauty is perfection, when in actuality beauty is what you see and feel right now. It's you! When we try to look like someone else, we lose our uniqueness. It is always better to be the best you rather than a poor imitation of someone else. Don't look at others and think, "If only I had…" or, "If I only I were…" But think about who you are and the many blessings you have received. We often forget that it is not the bag, shoes, or man that makes us valuable, but our strength and courage. We show our strength as women when we can say, "No, I am not perfect, but I am still beautiful." It's important we take the spotlight off of obtaining physical perfection and place it on valuing who we are right now. We are the real thing. We are beautiful.

Blog Post: Twinkle, Twinkle, Little Star

I wish I had everything I needed to do everything I want to do. I wish I had a team of assistants who could do all the things I dread doing. I wish I had the money to open up a grand office building.

Wait for it. Wait for it.

Okay, I had to stop waiting for it because in the real world where you and I live, we can't afford to wish on a star for things to happen. We have to start putting in the work to see change in our lives. And let me tell you, nothing comes easy. Anything worth having must be worked for in relationships, careers, and finances. You have to use what you have to get what you want. You have skills you are not using and opportunities you are not exploring because you are waiting for everything to be "right" or for the "perfect" timing.

But we can't wait for everything to be perfect. We have to dig into our bag of "what we have" to create "what we want." This may mean taking smaller steps than the big ones you prefer. It may take you longer to finish a project than you would like but at least you are not waiting. You are utilizing all of your resources to make your dreams come true.

COMMENTARY

Wow, that was a powerful blog post. At that time I was wishing for this and hoping for that. The truth is that wishing and waiting get us into so much trouble because they prevent us from achieving our goals. I remember pouting and wondering why it seemed things were working out for everyone except me. Then I figured out I have to stop watching everyone else and start focusing on my journey. I had to start using my resources to create the life I wanted.

In this life we must be willing to use what we have to move beyond our circumstances. If you want it, you can have it, but you have to be willing to work hard for it.

Secret Six: Move beyond Your Circumstances

How High Can You Go?

If you can visualize the life you want, then you can start making plans to move past your circumstances. We have to stop making excuses about what we don't have and start executing plans with what we do have.

The phrase, "Use what you have to get what you want," is usually thought of in a negative way. But, I want to bring a positive light to this statement. For me, using what you have to get what you want is about overcoming your circumstances to create the life you desire. If you look at your life right now there are steps you can take that will put you on the path to making your dreams come true. Maybe the steps you are able to take now are small but it is okay as long as you are moving in the right direction. It is important to remember that it takes time to make our dreams come true.

When you hear success stories, people often leave out all the dead ends and struggles that led to their success. There's no such thing as an overnight success. We must be willing to work hard if we desire a better life. I have talked with some women who don't want to take the next step in reaching their goals because they feel it isn't big enough or will not put them exactly where they want to be. But we must understand that every step is not going to be a defining moment or go exactly as planned. Some steps are meant to be small and serve as a foundation for those big steps.

Don't sit still waiting on the next big opportunity; start taking advantage of those opportunities available right now. We are smart and capable women who have the power to achieve our goals. There is no need for us to wait around for happiness when we have the power to make ourselves happy. We don't have to think, "I'll be happy if my boss gives me a promotion," or, "I'll be happy if he asks me to get married." Yes promotions and marriage are great but they shouldn't be the determining factors to say if you are happy or not.

It is our responsibility to go after our dreams, despite rejection and disappointment. We have to get off the emotional roller coaster that we ride when we give others the power to determine how we feel about ourselves. Sometimes things will not work out the way we think they should, but that doesn't mean we are failures. It just means we have to go back to the drawing board and think of other ways to use what we have to get what we want.

The essence of a strong woman is that she never gives up. We don't play dirty because we don't have to; our talents and skills speak for themselves. We don't have to kick and scream to be notice because our confidence tells everyone we are there when we walk into a room.

If you have given anyone or anything other than yourself the power to control your emotions, life, or destiny, then now is the time to take it back. It's time to stop allowing other people's decisions to determine what you are going to do with your life. Once you make the decision to take control of your own happiness, nothing will be able to stop you from achieving your goals. You are going to know how to get up, dust yourself off, and keep knocking on doors until the right one opens.

No one else can stop you from achieving your dreams unless you allow them to. Yes, somebody can make a decision and disappoint you, but at the end of the day, you have to decide whether or not you are going to move forward or stay complacent. You determine how high you can go in life.

Exercise 9: Use What You Have to Get What You Want

Use the following exercise to start your action plan to achieve your goals. These steps may not be where you ideally want to start, but they are steps that will allow you to take action today instead of waiting any longer to transform your dreams into reality.

○ **Goal:**

_____

_____

_____

○ How long has this been a goal for you?

_____

_____

_____

○ What are your challenges?

_____

_____

_____

○ What resources do you have today that can be utilized to put you on the path of accomplishing your goal?

_____

_____

_____

○ Using those resources what is one step you can take today? Remember, this does not have to be a huge step. As long as you are making positive changes you are on the right track.

_____

_____

_____

○ What are three actions you can take this week that will begin the change process in your life?

_____

_____

_____

Blog Post: Do you understand the words that are coming out of my mouth?

Yes, Ms. Professional, I understand the words, but your actions are saying something totally different. You say you are professional, but you are never on time. You dress for work as if you are going to the gym. You don't even have business cards.

And as for you, Ms. Diva, who always has the latest fashions and gadgets, why are you still in debt? Why don't you have a savings account? Better yet, why are you still living with your parents?

And I can't forget Ms. Perfect, always turning her nose up at others, passing judgment and has it all together. But why are you still running behind Mr. So-and-So? Why are you crying at home alone? Why are you wishing every day you could change your life but are afraid of what other people might say?

Why are we saying one thing and doing another?

COMMENTARY

I remember when I learned this the hard way. I was in the hair salon, and everyone was talking about their childhood and going to church. I joined in, talking about my experiences. I said, "I believe children should go to church. It gives them value and character." Now that I look back, I know I should have just kept my mouth closed!

One of the ladies in the salon—there is always one—asked me how often I went to church. I said I went to church when I was off from work and that sometimes I was so tired from working that I didn't go to church on Sunday. Before I got the words out of my mouth, she stated, "Well, your brother probably does not get to participate in a lot of church activities."

I responded by saying no, because of my schedule, we didn't participate as much as we should. As you can imagine, the longer the conversation went on, the more I felt like a hypocrite. Here I was saying how important church was for children, and I had not made it a priority. Yes, I was busy, but I was making time for the salon. It made me think about my words and actions and how they did not align. The conversation gave me new insight into the gap between my words and my actions, and needless to say, I had some work to do. That day I learned a valuable lesson, to always say what I mean and mean what I say.

7

Secret Seven: Align Your Actions with Your Words

Say What You Mean and Mean What You Say

"Actions speak louder than words." Remember, your goal is to be beautiful inside and out, and in order to do that, your actions must line up with your words. If you say you have control over your life, then you should not be having an emotional breakdown every week. If you say you are minding your own business, you have no time to be gossiping about what someone else is doing in his or her life. If you say you want to be successful, then you don't have time for spending every weekend in a club, talking on the phone all night, or lying on the couch watching television. There is nothing wrong with going out, talking on the phone, or watching television, but these activities should not interfere with you achieving your goals. If they are, then limit them. The club, the phone, and the television will still be there after you fulfill your dreams.

We all feel stuck sometimes but if you tell me the same story and excuses about why you can't step forward year after year, then I have to believe the problem lies in your efforts. As women, we don't have time for excuses. We don't have time to sit around hoping for something to change. We have to start standing up for who we are, what we want, and where we are going. Speaking our minds is generally frowned upon in our society, especially for women. If a woman is vocal about who she is and what she wants, and if she demands respect, then she is judged as being too aggressive, accused of trying to be like a man, or labeled a feminist or even a bitch. However, we have to move past what people may say or think of us if we want to be successful. As long as we are doing what we are supposed to do the right way, then people can just say what they will.

Keeping It Real, for Real

Effective communication is a beautiful part of being a confident woman. Being able to say what we mean and mean what we say is where the phrase "keeping it real" was probably derived. However, I have witnessed some women take this phrase to an entirely different level. "Keeping it real" should not be used as a cover-up for acting immature, disrespectful, or just plain out of control. You can keep it real and remain in control at the same time. You can get angry and upset without yelling and screaming. You can disagree with someone without putting your hands on them.

And let's just clear this up right now: if you are in public acting like a fool, you are not keeping it real. You are embarrassing yourself, the one who raised you, your children, your family, and all the women in the world who know how to act. I know sometimes people push our buttons intentionally, and sometimes unintentionally, but the only person we can control is ourselves.

Now, say it with me, "The only person I can control is myself." You must believe this and embrace it in your life in order to control your actions.

When I go to work, I am faced with different people with different personalities, objectives, backgrounds, and cultures. Not everyone will agree with me, and I may not agree with everyone else, but I must treat everyone with respect. No situation is bad enough to excuse instances of you acting immaturely in public. A strong, confident woman can keep her cool even when someone else's behavior is not acceptable.

When I hear a woman talking about fighting or cursing another woman out because of something she said, I get confused. What is she going to tell her daughter after the fight is over? How is she going to go to work the next day? What is worth fighting with another woman about? And then I realize there's no need to be confused because this kind of behavior will never make sense.

And let's talk about women who fight over men. I must say that if you find out your man has been cheating with another woman, your problem is with your man. Yes, she was wrong, but you are the one who had the commitment with him. Fighting the other woman is not going to resolve his infidelity. Why would you fight over a man who is disrespecting and cheating on you? When women fight, scream, and curse to keep their men, it shows me they don't have any confidence that their feelings will be heard. So, they use the most outrageous ways to get their feelings acknowledged. However, nothing results from drama but more drama.

Drama is not the key to getting heard; saying what you mean and meaning what you say is the key. Standing up and saying, "Cheating on me is not okay, so I am leaving," is more powerful than fighting and arguing. Stating in a staff meeting, "These are the things I see that need to be changed," is more constructive than gossiping about your coworker or manager. When we communicate our beliefs and stand behind them with our actions, we reveal our confidence in who we are. One of the most important components of beauty is confidence in our beliefs. It stands out more than any physical characteristic. When we are confident in what we believe, others cannot manipulate us into believing something else. This is important in intimate, family, and career relationships. People notice when you know who you are and can stand strong behind your beliefs without disrespectful behavior.

Speak Up

The confidence to speak your mind allows you to take action and remove yourself from situations that aren't the best for you. For example, sometimes we stay in relationships too long because we don't communicate our feelings. Sometimes we limit ourselves professionally because we hide our skills and abilities. We feel like, "Oh, it's not going to do any good. Maybe things will just get better in time." Every time you don't speak up for yourself, you internalize that as a failure. Which means your insecurity gets deeper and the fear of speaking up for yourself gets greater. This is like consistently taking steps backward in your life. When you don't communicate, then you're losing power over your life and giving it to somebody else.

Regardless of how others treat you, your silence says, "You know what's best for me. So you go ahead and make the choices for my life, and I'll just suffer the consequences of it." Those choices may not be what you want, but your silence stamps approval on them. If you don't speak up for yourself, you begin to teach people to speak for you and that is a big mistake. Speak up for yourself; be confident in who you are.

Don't go along with the crowd just because it is the easy thing to do. Stand up and be the best you.

Exercise 10: Align Your Actions with Your Words

In this exercise I want you answer the following questions after you think of a situation when you behaved in a way that did not align with the person you say you are.

○ When did you lose control of your actions?

_____

_____

○ In that situation, were you trying to control someone else's words, thoughts, or actions?

_____

_____

○ Looking back on the situation now, what should you have done differently?

_____

_____

○ Did you apologize for your actions?

_____

_____

○ How can you make sure you do not lose control of your actions in the future?

_____

_____

Blog Post: Lights, Camera, Action ... Let the Games Begin

"Who's hot and who's not?"
"Who's got it, who doesn't?"
"You're in, you're out."
"Why are we competing?"
"We are all hot, we all got it, and we all are in!"

Today it seems as if some women are competing for the "top spot" and don't care who they have to push aside, knock down or completely destroy to get there. Why are we competing for something we can all have...success. It does not matter who gets there first or gets the most recognition. What matters is that we all accomplish success with integrity. When we look at each other we should see a glimpse of ourselves because as women we have a special connection. We are connected through our struggles, our strength and our ability to love wholeheartedly. We can understand each other's fears and know what it's like to achieve something that everyone said we couldn't.

So why not embrace each other instead of breaking each other down. All we see on television are reality shows about women fighting each other over men, past relationships, you-said-she-said, and the status quo. Is this the only way we know how to get our point across? Are we not mature and confident women? I say we are and that it is time we move away from preying on each other's weaknesses and begin celebrating our strengths. When we know who we are we don't have to compete with each other. We can be confident in who we are, what we have, and where we are going. Yes, wanting more is great, but not just to outshine someone else.

COMMENTARY

Bravo, bravo!

I remember when I wrote this blog post. There were so many television shows that portrayed women as negative people who could only disagree by yelling, cursing and fighting. I couldn't understand what would make women want to hurt each other. Was the hostility really about what "she did" or what "she said?" Or was it something deeper? After talking with other women, it appears it is something deeper. The misunderstanding is that in order to be successful, we have to have a knock out, drag out fight against each other because there is only one "top spot." However, the reality is your success is not dependent on what someone else does. Focusing on running your own race and not trying to beat each other to the finish line is what places you on the path to success. Remember your success and my success are not mutually exclusive; there is enough happiness for all of us.

8

SECRET EIGHT: STOP COMPETING

Life Is Not a Competition

Everywhere you look you see news and advertisements about the latest fashion trends, hairstyles, and makeup. It's as if they are saying, "Hurry up and get these jeans before she gets them," and, "Hurry up and get this bag before she gets it," and even, "Hurry up and get this man before she gets him." However, if we're not careful, our actions and purchases can become no longer our preferences but about outshining someone else. We may not like the bag, house, or clothes that someone else has, but because they are getting attention we go out and get the same thing.

Being successful is not about competing with other women, but about allowing your light to shine so that you can inspire other women. We can't walk around with our nose up in the air as if we are better than others. No, we should not dim our light for others, but we also should not start flashing it just to get noticed.

Acting as if we are better than other women stops the communication between us and continues our mental and social competition mindset. Some women do have more money, prestige, and power than others, but we all put our panties on the same way. We feel that revealing our imperfections is a sign of weakness, though in reality the opposite is true. When we start to communicate honestly, we will find out that we have more in common than we thought. Hiding our true selves and acting like Ms. Perfect is a red flag which indicates that we are not confident about who we are.

We have to realize that Ms. Perfect is a made-up character created by advertising executives. We will never look like the model because the model does not look like the model. We are knocking down other women trying to reach something that is not a reality. Clearly, there is nothing wrong with taking care of your appearance, but our appearance does not define our character.

Now is the time when we stand together without judgment and allow ourselves to encourage each other again. Some women do so much finger-pointing, backstabbing, and man grabbing that they have lost themselves. We no longer understand the importance of sisterhood because we are too busy trying to out-dress, out-sing, or out-dance other women. Why can't we all be fabulous? Why can't I rock my style and you rock yours? We don't all have to look the same; we are different and our differences are beautiful. I don't care if your hair is a weave or not, and if your bag is authentic or a knockoff. If you are rocking it, then more power to you. But please know that looking your best and having what you want in life are not about competition. Trends go in and out, and you don't want to find yourself with a closet full of clothes but empty on the inside.

You have to learn to travel your own path. Somebody may already have their degree or their dream job. They may already be married and have the life they want. You don't need to keep their pace or follow in their footsteps. You're going to get where you need to be in your own time. There's no need to rush it. There's no need to become envious of other people's success.

Timelines are different for everyone. My life path and experiences will be different from yours. You can't compare your current situation with mine. However, if I am in a place you desire to be then you should be honest with yourself. Being honest allows you to say, "that's something that I want," and take steps to make that happen for you. But remember that your life is going to take you on your own unique path. Your end result may not look exactly like mine, but it will still be awesome. If you are motivated and if you have your goals in place, your dreams will come true. It's not about getting everything right now. It's about putting in the work, being patient, and watching your dreams manifest in time.

There's no rush. There's no competition.

Not a Secret, Just a fact!
Baby, You Are a Firework

Do you feel it? Do you feel the light burning inside you, fighting to get out, fighting to shine? Well, let it out. Don't fight it any longer.

Do you remember being a kid and going to see the fireworks on the 4th of July? I can remember waiting in anticipation, trying to guess what color the next one would be, and they were always better than I imagined. Whether we were watching with family or friends, we all wanted to see which firework would go the farthest and make the loudest noise.

With that memory in mind, I want you to think of yourself as a firework. Every day can be your 4th of July if you wake up with anticipation of all the possibilities that await you. With enough excitement, you can shoot past the moon and stars and make colors the world has never seen before.

You have a distinct capability that allows you to light up everything you touch. You no longer should feel the need to cover up your greatness. It does not matter if you are single, a stay-at-home mother, a politician, or teacher. You can make changes in your life so that your light can shine wherever you go. I'm not trying to say that the sky will always be clear. On the journey to your destiny there will be some rain and even some thunderstorms. You may feel alone and want to stop trying to make your dreams come true.

Remember that the reason you are a firework is not because of what you have or what you've accomplished, but because of your strength to endure hardships. We will all have times when we feel high and times when we feel low, but we should never count ourselves out just because challenges get in our way. As long as we remain determined to achieve our goals we can always dust ourselves off and keep moving towards our destiny.
You are brighter than the stars that shine above, stronger than the mountains in your view and more precious than all the diamonds.
You are a firework.

Blog Post: Mountain, I Say Move, Please?

Mountain, why won't you move? We have been over this same issue so many times. Do you not understand that you are keeping me from my destiny? What is that you say? I keep coming to you?

Oh, no. Don't blame this on me. I am always minding my own business, and when I look up there you are right smack in the middle of me and where I am going. So I will ask you nicely, move, please move and don't come back.

COMMENTARY

It was ridiculous. I kept going around the same mountain of issues, mistakes and challenges. I remember promising myself over and over again that I would never again be back at the same place. Before I knew it I was facing the same mountain again. I would wonder how could this happen. When I got so tired of wasting my time, effort, and energy, I started looking at my journey and the things that were hindering me. I realized I would never confront my challenges. I would just push them to the side and hope they would go away. My thought process was that I didn't have time to deal with it, but the truth was I would have to deal with it sooner or later.

Now I confront my challenges head-on because I can't afford not to. I would rather face the mountain now than to continue going around it. I have a destiny to get to and I have no time to waste.

Secret Nine: Confront your Challenges

Challenges Are Made to Make You Stronger

What do you do when there is an obstacle between you and your dreams? You do what you were born to do: **shine**. Don't get scared or worried. Just look at that challenge and say, "Bring it." Yes, you have to confront the challenge because the more time you allow it to linger in your life, the farther it pushes you from your dreams. I look at challenges as a way to become better and sharpen my skills because with every challenge comes a good lesson.

Let's say you have a dream of going backpacking across Europe, and every month you have decided to save $100 but month after month, you are unable to set aside that money. You start realizing that you don't even have enough money for regular monthly bills, and you have no idea where your money is going. Instead of looking at the situation and recognizing it as a challenge that needs to be addressed and resolved, some women would continue on the same path, hoping they'll have the money next month. However, if you merely ignore the problem and do not change what you're doing, the same thing is going to happen next month. Before you know it, time will fly and you'll still be struggling to save money, and you'll be no closer to your dream of traveling to Europe.

How to Make Challenges Work for You

Sometimes you may look at a challenge and say, "It wasn't my fault." And maybe it wasn't your fault, but because it has become a challenge for you in accomplishing your goals you must make a plan to overcome it. What are you going to do? Complain all day about how somebody messed up your life? And then what? The challenge will still be there, so why not take a deep breath and make a plan that will help you to overcome your challenge. We have no time to wait for someone to come and save the day; we have to become our own heroes. We can put on our superwoman cape and do extraordinary things.

When I was in college, I had to face a challenge that almost prevented me from graduating on time. When I was registering for classes for my senior year, I thought I had everything figured out. I planned out my schedule for the fall and spring semester knowing I needed just a few more classes to finish my degree. According to my schedule, I'd have plenty of time to study and work, and everything would turn out perfectly, or so I thought.

Right before classes started I realized that one of the classes was no longer available. I became frustrated and panicked. Without that class, my whole plan went out the window. I spent a considerable amount of time pointing my finger and thinking

"Well, the school should have let me know. Someone should have told me. Why would they wait to the last minute? It's just not fair." After all that complaining, all that finger pointing, the real question struck me: Did I want to graduate on time? Did I still want to meet my long-term goal? My answer was yes, so it was up to me to figure out a plan to overcome my challenge. It came down to either taking an extra class in the spring or taking a summer class.

So, I added a class to the spring and moved around my work schedule. I didn't have as much down time, and I had more responsibility during the spring semester, but I stayed on track and graduated on time with flying colors, well, maybe just with colors!

If your intention is to overcome challenges that come up, unexpected situations will not push your life into chaos.

Once you've overcome a challenge, you should celebrate the fact that you did so. Often we just keep going without stopping to give ourselves credit for working so hard. You should be proud of yourself. Each and every challenge you face and overcome is an accomplishment. Not only did you stay on track, but you're also closer to your long-term goal. That's a big deal, and celebrating will help keep you motivated and excited to continue in your journey.

Exercise 11: Confront Your Challenges

You will have challenges, but there are ways in which you can use your challenges to make you stronger. In the following exercise, think of a challenge you are facing right now and go through the steps to overcome it.

○ What is the current challenge?

_____

_____

○ Why did the challenge occur?

_____

_____

○ Are you willing to accept responsibility for the challenge?

_____

_____

○ What action do you need to take to overcome the challenge?

_____

_____

○ How can you be proactive to stop the challenge from returning?

_____

_____

Blog Post: Settle? Who Does That?

Unfortunately we do. I, you, and many other single women settle for careers, relationships and finances that are nowhere near what we deserve. We talk our way out of going after what we want because we are so afraid of failing. The questions of "what if" plague our mind. What if I am not good enough? What if he doesn't love me? What if I get criticized?

But what about the other "what if's?" What if you exceed all of your expectations? What if he loves you more that you could imagine? What if you get a standing ovation? You never thought about those scenarios?

We are in control of the actions we take and how we live our lives. Yes, we are all dealt different cards, but we must learn how to use those cards to create the life we desire. You may not have a winning hand to start, but keep your head in the game of life. Watch, learn and practice, and the odds will start turning in your favor. Why should you settle for less when you can have more? This is your life, your rules, so don't stand by and watch your dreams drift away in the distance. Run, power walk, do whatever you can do to grab them.

Wake up and see your future; see the possibilities whistling to get your attention. It is time to get up and live the life you were created to have.

COMMENTARY

I will be the first to admit that I have settled for less than I deserved on several occasions. Every time I have settled, I felt it. I felt I could do better. However, the fear of the "what if's" held me back from getting everything I wanted out of life. Settling is nothing to be ashamed of, but it is something we must stop doing immediately. Every time we settle, a little part of our voice gets silenced. And our voice is what makes us unique and powerful, so we must protect it at all times.

You don't have to settle. You can have the life you want if you just have patience with yourself. I am not telling you something I read somewhere, but something I know. I refuse to settle anymore because I am worth more. I am worth everything I can dream of. Yes, you will get scared and nervous on your journey to make your dreams come true, but keep going until you create the life you deserve.

10

Secret Ten: Don't Ever Settle

Get Strong, Get Confident, Get Courageous

When we were little girls, we would play dress up and confidently declare what we wanted to be when we grew up: a dancer, teacher, lawyer, astronaut, mother; our dreams were filled with color and excitement. We paid no attention to what other people thought or said about our dreams. We saw no limits in what we could become and were determined to prove our naysayers wrong. When we grew up, that passion and excitement disappeared for some of us. Bills, responsibilities and everyday pressures stole our focus. As a result, we found ourselves settling in an unhappy life.

When we settle we feel we can do better in a certain area of our life, but we don't go for it because we are too afraid that we won't succeed or lose what we already have. But what you don't realize is that what you are settling for doesn't compare to what you were created to do.

Yes, we have responsibilities, including the responsibility to ourselves to do everything possible to make our dreams come true. We may have to work while going back to school. We may have to start our business on the side while working full-time. And that's okay because our dreams are not going to just fall mysteriously into our laps. We have to work hard for what we want. We have to quit waiting for someone else to step in and make our dreams come true.

Being Right All the Time Isn't Right

I think a lot of times we settle or stay in a situation because we refuse or are scared to say we made a mistake. We do this in our relationships by refusing to admit we are involved with the wrong guy because we dismissed advice and red flags that showed he wasn't right for us. We then think "I'm going to stay in this relationship and try my best to change him."

Yet, the real reason you're staying in the relationship is that you don't want to admit you made a mistake. We're all going to make mistakes. That's part of life.

That's part of growing. When we're able to grow, we know that our self-worth doesn't have to be destroyed by mistakes. Every day is a new day to start over and make changes in our lives.

It happens in our career too. You may leave one job for another opportunity and think it will be the perfect career move. We think, "This is going to be perfect. I am not going to work weekends. I'm going to get home at a decent time. They promised me bonuses." Then you tell everybody about how great it's going to be: your coworkers, your family, and all your Facebook friends. But, when you finally get to the job, things aren't as great as you thought they would be. You don't get all the bonuses or time off that you thought you would get, and it turns out you're unhappy. You may think, "I'm just going to stay here, because it would be too embarrassing to go back and tell people I made a mistake."

Then you start trying to cover up your mistakes in your career and relationships, telling other people, "Yeah, my job is fine. Oh, no, my relationship is rosy. I love him. He loves me." We lie to ourselves and others because we're afraid to admit our mistakes. Understand that you're not perfect, you're going to make mistakes, and as soon as you come clean about it you'll relieve the pressure of trying to hold that imperfect situation together. You don't have to stay in a relationship when you are not happy or in a career where you are not progressing.

As women, we don't want to forget we have the right to change our minds. We don't have to be burdened with trying to make wrong choices right.

You deserve better.

Once we admit the mistake, then we can grow and move on. We can open up a dialogue with other women and empower them to do the same. You show the world through your example: "Hey, if you are in a broken relationship, you don't have to stay there. If you made a wrong move in your career or you want to try something else, you can do that. If your financial situation is not where you need it to be, you can ask for help.

We all have different experiences and skills that can help other women. You can show your friends and the women around you that they don't have to have it all together all the time. We can just be free to be ourselves and not settle for anything less than we deserve. Different experiences are going to push you and challenge you to be better. Make sure that the decisions you make are going to reflect the woman that you have become and not the woman you used to be. Don't make decisions based on your past. You evolve every day.

Sometimes it's hard to let go of the woman you were to make room for the woman you are now. However, we must realize what was good enough then is not good enough anymore. This realization helps you not to stay stuck in one place because you're scared of what might come in the future. It's like playing softball and staying frozen on first base so that no one can tag you out. You'd rather stay right where you are because there's no risk of getting hurt, no messy or risky sliding. But you miss all those possibilities for a home run! The truth is that there is more out there for you than you ever imagined. When you're at bat, everything is new and fresh. When you get to first base your perspective is a little different. By third base your viewpoint has changed again. You feel the breeze on your face and find strength to keep running. Once you reach home, that place where all your goals, dreams and aspirations are waiting for you, you realize it was all worth it. You realize the journey was worth the risk.

Exercise 12: Stop Settling

Write at the top of separate index cards: Relationships, Finances, and Career. For each area on the top of your index card, I want you to write if you are Settling or Not Settling and explain why. If there is an area you are settling in, I want you to make a plan to stop it immediately!

For example:

```
Relationships

Not settling:
     I deserve someone to love
        me and be committed.


```

```
Finances

Settling:
        Don't know how to
        stick with a budget.


```

```
Career
Settling:

        Scared to follow my passion.


```

Blog Post: I Think I Can. I Think I Can.

I am sitting here thinking of all the things I want to do, places I want to go, and people I want to inspire. As these exciting thoughts go through my mind there is one consistent thought of "I think I can." I hate to admit it but there is this little piece of doubt that sits in the back of my mind that asks, "Can you really do this?"

I respond, "I think I can," but the problem is that "I think" is no longer strong enough to move me towards making my dreams come true. "I think" keeps me stagnate, like keeping my foot on the brakes after the traffic light has turned green.

"I think" is making me more than cautious; it is making me fearful. So I have to change "I think" to "I know." I have to believe I can do it, that everything I've dreamed of is possible.

COMMENTARY

Sometimes the "I think I can" mentality tries to creep back in, but I quickly escort it out. I learned that "I think" is the same as "I doubt," and there is no room for doubting myself if success is my goal. I have confidence in my abilities, and that confidence is my motivation to transform my dreams into reality.

It seemed that all my statements at that time began with "I think," as in: "I think I want this," and "I think I can do that." Finally I realized "I think" was the problem. Enough of doubting myself...

Not a Secret: Just a Fact
You Can Change Your Life

If you think back over all the secrets and facts, one thing should be clear: you have the power to change your life. You now see the benefits of becoming confident in who you are and having an action plan for your future. I hope you are curious about all the possibilities awaiting you in your life. Most of all, I hope you learned that there is no reason for you to settle for less than you deserve.

In essence, we are all in this thing called life together. We should look to see how we can begin to help each other, serve our community, and become better individuals. If we have this perspective, when we reach success, we can bring someone else with us. When I inspire you, you become empowered. When you become empowered, you begin to live differently. By changing your life, you will inspire someone else, and the cycle of change starts again. It is not just about "if I make it," but "if I can use my success to inspire someone else to reach their goals." All of our strengths and talents were designed to come together and meet one common goal, which is to make the world a better place. We do that by discovering who we are and our purpose in life.

You see, the ideas that make you jump for joy may not excite me at all, but that's okay because our differences are what give us the ability to create change. While I am sleeping, you are writing and researching those ideas in your mind. While you are sleeping, I am creating ways for your ideas to have a breakthrough. Without each other our dreams have no life. So I have taken the first step . . . here I am: my secrets, thoughts, struggles and dreams are all before you. This is my way of helping you to join me in a place of success, not of having things, but of being true to yourself and living a life designed just for you.

Open your mind so that you can see all the possibilities awaiting you in the future. Allow your thoughts to take you on a colorful ride filled with success and happiness. You can do whatever you want, be whoever you want, and go wherever you want, but first and foremost you must determine your direction. It is always easier to walk in the direction that is most common and comfortable. But it takes courage to walk into the unknown with confidence that you will succeed. It is your decision to either settle for less or strive to achieve your dreams. No one can make this decision for you. You have to be the one who says, "Enough is enough. Okay is not good enough."

In love,

Suntia

More Blog Posts:
To Help You Leave The Past Behind
Leaving Your Relational Baggage At the Door

We are collectors.

Throughout our lives, we collect opinions, passions, memories and insights. We internalize these, and they become a part of how we act and react, what we say and how we say it, and the decisions we make. By the time we are adults, we have collected decades' worth of life-changing experiences. We are walking, talking assemblages of our past encounters.

And this includes trauma from our long-ago and not-so-long-ago relationships.

We carry with us the hurt from past intimate relationships as well as the pain from parents, siblings, friends and co-workers. This is what I call relational baggage. From my work with clients over the years, I know that many people lug a big, bulky pile of baggage around with them — into new romantic partnerships, new friendships, and new work environments. And that's when your troubling past comes back to disrupt your brand-sparkling-new relationships.

When you bring baggage into your new relationships, your partner's words and/or actions can become triggers for that past trauma. Take for example: If in the past you were lied to and cheated on, you will probably have your deception radar scanning at all times. If your partner is 30 minutes late, makes a complaint about you or goes out with his or her friends, you may be quick to assume that they don't love you and/or they are deceiving you.

I know you may say, "Well, Suntia, I just have trust issues." And my response is this: Deal with them by healing from them.

Healing For Real

Your trust issues should not be something your partner has to learn to adjust to. That's not fair. They didn't hurt you, they didn't leave, they did not cheat on you. They are only trying to love you, but you won't let them — because you are holding them accountable for what someone else did. Maybe it's not a past boyfriend, girlfriend, husband or wife. Your trauma may stem from something that happened as a child. Maybe your parents left you, so you now hover over your current partner because you fear they will leave.

But ask yourself this: What type of life are you living if you wake up everyday with fear that your beloved is going to leave? What type of life are you living if you are constantly plagued by paranoia that your partner will cheat or lie?

If we don't heal from past pain, our relationships can become war zones of fighting, miscommunication and loss of connection and intimacy. It is not our partner's responsibility to heal us; we must take the lead on that. Can our partners show us compassion, empathy and understanding for our pain? Oh yes! That makes a relationship real. When we can share our hurt with our partner without the expectation that they take on responsibility for it, that fosters intimacy on a whole other level.

Let It Go

I'm going to be honest with you. This is not going to be easy. Healing from the horrible things you experienced in the past will be a challenge. But every difficult step will be worth it, because one day you will be freed of the burden of this baggage. You will no longer relive the feelings, the fear, the anger that has been tormenting you for so long, and you will actually give yourself a shot at happily ever after.

This process is difficult because letting go can feel like you are letting someone off the hook, right?

But I can assure you that is far from the truth. I work diligently to show my clients that it does not matter who left you, who would not or could not love you, who hurt you. You have a choice to move forward. You have a choice to use that pain to fuel your purpose in life. We all have a journey in life filled with joy and pain, and they both equally shape who we are.

Having a parent leave you is heart shattering. I've been there. Having a person — a person you were going to spend the rest of your life with — betray you, it knocks the breath out of you. I've been there too. Having friends walk away from you in your time of need, it bring tears to your eyes. Again, I've been there too. But taking the time to heal from all that pain and coming out free and happy is priceless. I am there right now!

So, I can tell you from experience, the key to healing from relational baggage is to accept that someone you loved hurt you and to face that pain. You can never escape pain; you can mask it, and you can create defense mechanisms. But no matter what you do, the pain is still there just waiting for a chance to come out and heal.

And honestly, if you want to remain stuck in the past, you are the only one suffering. The person who hurt you? They have moved on. So, are you willing to let someone else have that power over your life?

Taking Back Your Power

You know that old saying, "The first step is admitting that you have a problem." Well, it is true. You need to realize and acknowledge that your past relationships are interfering with your current relationship. I usually have my clients observe their partner's actions and think to themselves, "If I didn't go through [enter past trauma here], would I feel like this or react like this?" This exercise brings your awareness to how the past influences your feelings and actions and how it is affecting your relationship.

Next, it is time to go through what I like to call "the differentiation process." This is where you begin to journal about your past experiences. Write down your partner's actions or words that trigger your pain, and then write down how your partner and the person who hurt you are different. I have my clients do this process until it is clear that their partner is different from the person who hurt them.

The process of healing from past relational hurt is different for all people. Some of my clients have gone through severe trauma, like sexual and physical abuse. Some of my clients have had parents abandon them. Some clients have gone through partners' betraying them. But I usually find that the differentiation process is a good first step in healing.

The Art of Letting Go: Reflection

Maybe it's work. You loathe the idea of walking into the office each morning, you can't stand your boss and the job is beyond boring. Or maybe it is your partner. You are constantly worried about saying the wrong thing or you have just grown so tired of being criticized. The emotional intimacy is disappearing and the physical intimacy is gone. Or maybe it's a friendship that has turned nasty, and yet you still answer her calls and spend time dealing with her drama.

To those bad relationships, bad jobs, bad life decisions, you say "it's just the way it is." Or you consider it a phase that will "hopefully improve." "Some day" you will move on, you keep telling yourself.

Over the years, I've worked with many people who struggle to say goodbye to the dysfunction in their lives. They are in a relationship, career, friendship or financial commitment, and they know it's time to let go, time move on. But they don't. They are fearful of what is next. Will they ever find someone who will love them the way they deserve? Will they ever have the career they desire? Will they be alone? That fear becomes debilitating. And they find themselves in the same situations over and over — because they are fearful of letting go of the familiar even if it does not make them happy.

That is why I am writing this series, which I am calling "The Art of Letting Go." I am separating it into five parts:

The Art of Letting Go: A 5-Part Series
1. Reflection: Learning who you are and who you want to be
2. Awareness: Understanding the changes that need to occur
3. Forgiveness: Making peace with your and others' mistakes
4. Acceptance: Leaving the familiar and embracing the unknown
5. Balance: Making steps 1-4 a part of your life; continuing to grow

Why is Letting Go Important?

The Art of Letting Go is about deciding to stop making the same mistakes and choosing to take a different path. It has been said that insanity is doing the same thing over and over and expecting a different result, and I totally agree. When we hold onto things that weigh us down, that negativity turns into baggage. The more baggage you have, the more it clouds your view and the more you feel like carrying that baggage around is the only way to live. Your baggage-cluttered perspective becomes the viewpoint from which you see the world.

But how can you have a positive outlook when all you see is negativity? The truth is, you can't.

That is precisely why you must learn what to hold onto and what to let go of. When that happens, your momentum increases, you feel lighter and, most of all, you know your worth. In life, we are all going through the growing pains of becoming the person we want to be. For some people, the pain is too much, and they give up. Instead of moving forward, they decide to stay stagnate and hold onto the very things that keep you down. If you can grasp one thing from this series, it is that in life we will have to let go of things, people and situations; when we understand and embrace this process, we allow ourselves to be free within. And when we are free within, that freedom to live life fully, spills into our families, relationships, career and finances.

I know letting go is painful and scary, but if you don't let go, you miss out on the life you always wanted, the life you deserve.

Let's Get Started: A Look at Reflection

Reflecting is a part of letting go because you must be able to know yourself — who you are and what you want — before you know what you need to let go of. For example, I know that I want to be happy and I want to have peace. If there is anything in my life that does not give me happiness and peace, then I need to let it go. If I am in a relationship that doesn't bring me peace or happiness, I'm kicking it to the curb. If my career is consistently stressing me out, good bye! If a family member drains my energy, I set boundaries to decrease the time I am around them. This is how I live. This is my life mantra, "Peace and happiness is where I reside this day and everyday of my life." Anyone who knows me, knows this is 100 percent true. But in order to do this, I must constantly reflect on myself and be present in the moment to know what I must let go of. Everyday, life gives you new relationships, opportunities and experiences, and it is up to you to decide what stays and what goes. There are situations that happen that we have no control over: our boss assigns us a big project at the last minute, our loved one passes away, we lose our job, our child gets sick. Those things we cannot control. Letting go is about changing the situations that we have the power to change, and reflection is the first step in the process.

It's simply about making the decision to move forward, to bet on yourself and to know that you can have the life you want. So many times, my clients will say, "I am tired of this relationship (or job or financial situation)." But when, I offer them solutions, they say, "Well, maybe where I am isn't so bad." You know why? It is easier to stay where you are than to move forward because moving forward takes courage and accountability. If you start owning your power and something goes wrong, then who can you blame? No one. You can't point the finger and say it's because "he hurt me" or "because she left me" or "because my mom did this" or "my dad said that." Because the truth is, it doesn't matter who left or who couldn't love you, you are responsible for your own life and actions. You are the one who decides how your story ends. And you likely want a happy ending to your story, right?

The Reflection Formula: How to Find Yourself
When it comes to this initial stage of letting go, I give my clients this little formula:
Discovering your dreams in life
+ Steps to make your dreams come true
÷ Courage
= Finding yourself

Self-reflection is the key to each variable in the equation. You need time alone, time to just be you, to dig deep and discover your dreams. What do you want? What puts a smile on your face? Does it sound a little selfish? Trust me, it is not selfish. It's self-awareness! How can you begin to create a healthy relationship, have a fabulous career and financial security if you don't know who you are? You need to get in touch with your inner wants and needs to find out what drives you.

What makes me a master at the art of letting go is that mantra I spoke about earlier: "Peace and happiness is where I reside this day and everyday of my life." During reflection, if I am confused about my next steps in life, I just think about my situation in terms of that mantra. If my reality and my mantra are in line, then I stick with it. If a part of my life is not reflective of my mantra, then I have to let it go. Generally speaking, I do not mind challenging myself, I do not mind the risk of failing, I do not even mind a little stress, but if it takes away my peace and happiness, that is where I draw the line.

So, what is your life mantra? During your moments of reflection you will discover a mantra for yourself, a personal motto that helps you stay focused on you. Create it, and stick with it. You can even add to it. Make it a fun way to reflect and a signal for when you need to let something or someone go.

Sometimes what we thought we wanted in life — a certain career path maybe or a relationship — is not really making us happy. When you reflect and when you are being totally honest with yourself, you can say, "I thought I wanted to do this, but I don't anymore," and then you change course. You do not have to feel defeated because you changed your goals, your wants or your needs. You should not stagnate because you are fearful of changing course. In case no one told you, you have the right to change your mind. Do you want to be on your deathbed with regrets? I know I don't. Life is too short. I want to live, make mistakes, change my mind and let go, so that I can love more, smile more, laugh more and feel more positivity.

Just look back over your life and think about all the things you wish you would have let go of sooner. Think about all the lessons you wished you would have learned from and then moved on. Now is the time to master it and live the life you always wanted.

The Art of Letting Go: Awareness

The Art of Letting Go: A 5-Part Series
1. Reflection: Learning who you are and who you want to be
2. **Awareness: Understanding the changes that need to occur**
3. Forgiveness: Making peace with your and others' mistakes
4. Acceptance: Leaving the familiar and embracing the unknown
5. Balance: Making steps 1-4 apart of your life; continue to grow

If you have already read about reflection, then you have likely spent some time contemplating what makes you happy in life...and what doesn't. Maybe you have reflected on your own hopes, dreams and standards, and you've developed a better relationship with yourself. Maybe you've thought about how fear is keeping you from moving on from unhealthy relationships, careers, financial situations or friendships. Maybe you even have your own mantra by now.

From Reflecting to Planning

Self-reflection is the first step of letting go because you find out who you are and who you want to be. Now that you clearly see the gap between your present state and your ideal self, you must create action steps to close that gap. I want to make it clear that awareness is not a one-time deal. You must remain aware every-day so that everyday you are moving forward to the life you want.

To reach your goals, envision the steps you need to take to be the person you would like to be. In other words, you must be aware of 1) your present reality, 2) what you want to happen in your future and 3) the changes that need to take place to get you there. Many people can easily reflect and daydream about their ideal life, but they do not plan the changes that take them from point A to point B.

For example, maybe you will see the difference between the woman you are (insecure) and the woman you want to be (confident), then you can determine what you need to do to close the gap. Maybe it's forgiving your dad for leaving you, taking an exercise class, attending church or standing up for yourself in your relationship.

Or maybe, when you self-reflect, you see the difference between the woman you are (working at a job you hate) and the woman you want to be (working in a ca-reer you love). Now through awareness, you can de-termine some actions steps of going back to school to receive a degree in business, reaching out to your sup-port system to help care for your child and start apply-ing for jobs that will allow you to get some experience while you get your degree. You see, awareness is creat-ing your design for change. However, you must contin-ue to stay aware everyday so you do not regress.

The Challenges of Plotting Change

Self-doubt is a big pitfall during the awareness process because you see all these steps that you must take and you think, "I can't do that! What will people say? What if I fail?" Then you just stop. It's easier to stop than to make all these changes, right? But once you are aware, it is tough to go back to living life as you were. You have heard the longing inside of yourself for more. You know who you want to be.

That is why most people don't like the awareness process. It is when things get real. All of a sudden you have given yourself the power to ultimately design your life, and that can be scary. You are completely in control, and you cannot blame anyone else for your future.

But if you continue to stay stagnant — aware that positive change is possible but too afraid to take the needed steps — bitterness will grow. You will begin to resent others who had the courage to move forward. We often hear about "haters," and I truly believe that haters are people who did not have the courage to go after their dreams. They are angry at those of us who do. So don't be a hater, close the gap and make your dreams come true.

Finding Your Strength

When self-doubt comes or when change seems too daunting, say a affirmations like, "If I keep moving forward I cannot fail. I am strong. I deserve to be happy." I love affirmations, and my clients have grown to love them too because we have to learn how to motivate ourselves. We have to learn that if we don't believe in ourselves then who will?

And the truth is that change is going to happen. Either you face it willingly or you cry and scream and pout about it. But it is going to happen. Knowing this, why not use your strength and roll with it? Why not take the initiative and take control of change? Before someone tells you that you have the potential to get a better job, you know it! Before someone tells you your boyfriend sucks and you can do better, you know it! Before someone tells you that you should go back to school to become a teacher because you love to teach, you know it! So why wait? Make the necessary changes now; let's rock our life now.

I know letting go is scary and painful, but it is the kind of fear that energizes you to keep moving because you know you are looking for more. This is also where affirmations can help. I cannot say it enough: I have affirmations all over the place because even the most optimistic person has down days. Affirmations allow you to remember who you are and who you want to be.

The Art of Letting Go: Forgiveness

We all have regrets: I should have quit my job years ago... I would be so much more successful if my parents were supportive of me... I could be happily married by now if I'd broken up with him years ago.

Do any of those sound familiar? During the process of letting go, you have been thinking about who you are and who you want to be, and you have looked at all the things you need to change in your life to reach your goals. And during these moments of reflection and planning, I know you have thought about what has hindered you from being your ideal self.

That's why the third step in The Art of Letting Go is forgiveness:

The Art of Letting Go: A 5-Part Series

1. Reflection: Learning who you are and who you want to be
2. Awareness: Understanding the changes that need to occur
3. **Forgiveness: Making peace with your and others' mistakes**
4. Acceptance: Leaving the familiar and embracing the unknown
5. Balance: Making steps 1-4 a part of your life; continue to grow

Regret and Blame

Now that you know what you need to change in your life, you must forgive yourself and others for all the shouldas, wouldas, couldas. Why? Well, regret is the secret weapon of self-doubt, and self-doubt is a barrier to positive change. The more regret and the more blame you internalize, the harder it is to progress forward.

Regret is sly. It can sneak in and trap you before you even know it. You begin to think about all the things you could have done differently, and at first, you are simply trying to understand what went wrong. But then thoughts begin to turn negative. That is because you have not forgiven yourself. Without forgiveness, you start to emotionally beat yourself down, and that ultimately leads to self-doubt. Or you may be blaming someone else for your missed opportunities. Holding onto a lot of blame can also leave you debilitated— because you are spending all of your energy focused on your anger, resentment and bitterness toward someone else. The person who hurt you is off living their life, and they may or may not remember what they even did to you. So who is ultimately suffering? You. Because you cannot move on...until you forgive.

Blame and guilt ensure that you are stuck in the past. They keep you reliving the same mistakes over and over again. Anytime you get a glimpse of what your life could be, you are knocked down by your past. Many times we try to hold onto bad memories as a badge of honor: "I am like this because I went through X, Y or Z." But you will soon realize that this is not a badge of honor. There is no honor in allowing someone else's actions to dictate your future.

Forgiveness in Action

If you look at your life and see some form of dysfunction, I guarantee that there is a lack of forgiveness. That is why you cannot let go of the dysfunction. The dysfunction is the piece of you that still hates how you were brought up, and you cannot move past it because you have not forgiven your parents. The dysfunction is the piece of you that regrets that you were a teen parent, and you cannot move past it because you have not forgiven yourself. If you keep asking yourself why drama follows you everywhere, it's because you have not forgiven yourself and/or someone else. You have the choice to not let your past determine how you live your life.

When you look at your past and remember the people who have hurt you and the wrong decisions you made, instead of getting angry or sad, choose to hold no grudges. Forgive them, let it go and the universe will send you opportunities, people and abundance to help you heal, to start you on your path of changing your life. It is all a part of your journey. It is all motivation to move toward the life you want and the life you deserve.

The Challenge of Forgiveness

The hardest part of forgiving others is that it can seem as though you are letting people off the hook for hurting you. But forgiveness is not about them. It is about you. It is about letting go of the anger that remains from what they did to you. It's about freedom.

On the other hand, the challenging part of forgiving *yourself* is overcoming the self-punishment instinct. You think that because of what you have done you do not deserve to be happy. But I want to ask you: Why shouldn't you be happy? If mistakes were the determining factor for happiness, then no one would be happy. We all have made and will continue to make mistakes. It is life. It's part of being human. No matter how bad you think your mistakes are, they still do not have the power to take away your happiness — unless you give it away. You are worthy. You deserve to move forward.

We do the best we can in life, in relationships and in our careers, and even our best is not perfect. We still make wrong decisions. We can always look back and say, "I should have taken a right instead of left." But we can't go back in the past and change anything. We can start today, in the present moment, to change our lives.

Living Forgiveness

I once heard that diversity does not build character; adversity does. This has been true in my life. It is easy to move forward and to be successful when you are surrounded by people who think like you, who treat you well and who adore you. But what happens when you are faced with people who do not think like you? Who do not treat you well? Do you stop going after your dreams? Or do you keep going no matter who likes you, who is clapping for you, who is hating on you?

You see, this step of letting go is not just about absolving the mistreatment of your past; it is about shaking off the constant criticism, negativity and drama that comes our way each day. It is about keeping your eyes on that image of you as your ideal self and not letting anyone else bring you down or allow you to stray from your goals. you forgive and you move on - this is essential to a life of peace and freedom.

The Art of Letting Go: Acceptance

You've heard it before: The truth will set you free.

In life, dishonesty is not just about the little white lies we tell to our friends ("No, really, you look great in that dress!") or co-workers ("I'm definitely *not* looking for a new job. I love it here."). Dishonesty is also the little white lies that we tell ourselves and the big, broad falsehoods that are so ingrained in our minds that we've almost convinced ourselves they are real. You know, those lies. The ones that you tell yourself to keep the peace in your household, that ensure you are not rocking the boat and that means life stays exactly the same. These are the lies that keep you from being the person you want to be.

That's why the fourth step in the process of letting go is acceptance of the truth.

The Art of Letting Go: A 5-Part Series

1. Reflection: Learning who you are and who you want to be
2. Awareness: Understanding the changes that need to occur
3. Forgiveness: Making peace with your and others' mistakes
4. **Acceptance: Leaving the familiar and embracing the unknown**
5. Balance: Making steps 1-4 a part of your life; continue to grow

During the process of letting go, you have been thinking about who you are and your goals, and you have looked at all the aspects you need to change in your life to reach your goals. You've forgiven yourself and let go of the guilt and blame that has kept you from moving forward with your life. The previous steps have helped us to get rid of the clutter in our minds and hearts, allowing us to see where we want to go and who we want to be.

And now is the time to see the truth, accept it and actually move forward.

Acceptance in Action

It comes down to this: If you do not accept your reality, then your status quo revolves around avoiding the truth — the bad relationships, the professional unhappiness, the financial troubles, the family drama. It means you stay stagnate and hold on to the things that are keeping you down, ensuring you will never be the person you want to be.

However, acceptance means that you embrace each moment. You do not resist what is happening or what has happened — but you allow the reality of your situation to be exactly what it is. There is no justification, there are no excuses. There is simply an understanding that what has happened or what is happening is not a reflection of who you are or who you want to be. It is just an experience you are going through. And just like all experiences, it too shall pass.

This is a pivotal part of letting go because you cannot let go of what you have not accepted. Denial ensures that you hold onto your drama, unhappiness and dysfunction. That's because you are still trying to make the bad into something good. You are essentially trying to fit a square peg into a round hole, and it's not moving. Of course it wouldn't. You cannot simply ignore the dysfunction in your life and hope that it turns into something functional.

Some people may think that if they avoid an issue, then their avoidance makes it less true/real. But in reality, avoidance makes the issue worse, and it begins to cause other problems in your world. It envelops you.

When you stifle all of the emotions associated with an issue/challenge/experience, it can cause a breakdown, a meltdown, a whole lot of anger and constant unhappiness. When you avoid the reality of your marital problems, you become a human teakettle, and eventually your bitterness will loudly bubble to the surface. When you avoid your financial problems, they get worse, the stress becomes all encompassing and you may let it begin to impact other areas of your life, including your relationships and professional life.

You know that time you yelled at your daughter, your son, your husband or your subordinate at work over something small? I can guarantee that deep down you know that was more about the personal issues you were avoiding than it was about their small transgression.

Your Moment of Truth

If you really want to become a master of letting go, then you must learn to accept everything as it is. Many people say, "How can I accept them hurting me... getting fired... losing my house?" Acceptance does not mean that you don't take action, "Well, that's just how it is." It means you take in the truth of what has happened, process it, acknowledge how it has affected you and then move forward.

I've said it before: If you do not accept the truth, then you will never move forward. The truth can be a starting line to the future you want. It's the before picture. It's your motivation to become the person you want to be, to achieve your dreams, to make your reality into something you've always wanted.

And it gives you the incentive to face the unknown, and say, "I never want to put myself in that situation again."

The Challenges of Acceptance

During the acceptance process, you may be stricken by what I like to call, "Feel good acceptance." That means that while things are good in your life, you can accept the hurt and pain that someone caused you. You can accept that you were fired without a cause or that your father was not there for you when you were a child.

But as soon as something goes wrong, you begin to bring up everything bad that has happened in your life.

When the going gets tough, you are once again a victim of past crimes, and the anger and bitterness that you had left in the past begin to resurface.

To avoid this, you must remember to tell yourself that no one else's actions should affect what you do for yourself. They only have the power to hold you back if you give it to them. Knowing this will allow you to fully accept your present and past.

The Freedom That Comes With the Truth

I know change is scary and admitting your own wrongdoings and the faults of others can be difficult. But acceptance takes away the burden of what went wrong, who left, what mistakes you made, etc. It lifts all of this off your shoulders. It allows you to step outside of the blame game, the guilt game and be free to change your life.

So many people wear the burden of "making it right" or "understanding why." They seek some sort of understanding: why your dad left, why your husband cheated, why you never went to college. But the truth is that you may never make it right and you may never understand their/your actions. Acceptance allows you to take the energy from that and put it toward creating the life you want.

I know some situations are incredibly difficult to accept because to accept may mean your partner lied or your friend was not there for you. But what is the alternative? Do you want to let their actions or your actions keep replaying in your mind? Do you want to keep making the same mistakes? Why not accept it? Why not feel your emotions and heal from your pain?

When you accept your past and present, it allows you to gain perspective, be confident in your decisions and begin to take a step toward change.

The Art of Letting Go: Balance

Veni, vidi, vici. I came, I saw, I conquered.

As I write the final piece in my series on The Art of Letting Go, that's what my mind keeps going back to: You came, you read and with hope, you are conquering. It's empowering for me to think about all the successes you will have because of your ability to let go of the elements in your life that aren't working, that are holding you back, that are causing you to make the same mistakes over and over.

We've covered a lot of ground in this series. During the process of letting go, you have learned who you are and what you want, and you have discovered what you need to change in your life to reach your goals. You have focused on forgiveness and freed yourself of the guilt and blame that has kept you from moving forward with your life. All of the steps have led you to this point: to balance.

The Art of Letting Go: A 5-Part Series

1. Reflection: Learning who you are and who you want to be
2. Awareness: Understanding the changes that need to occur
3. Forgiveness: Making peace with your and others' mistakes
4. Acceptance: Leaving the familiar and embracing the unknown

5. Balance: Making steps 1-4 a part of your life; continue to grow

Your New Balancing Act

The balance step is the best step. Because it's about enjoying each day and taking the time to see yourself as you are. You are taking all that you've learned from the previous steps and integrating them into your way of thinking. Everyday you are reflecting, you are staying aware and you are forgiving. You are not fighting against your history or your present. You are accepting of all aspects of your life. You have a plan in place to change the things you want to change, and you are working toward your goals. You are prepared to take some risks and spread your wings.

When you have balance, you are not rushing toward the finish line of life, stressed out and nervous. At the same time, you are not stagnant. You are enjoying the journey with peace and happiness. You are a bit like the tortoise in the tale of The Tortoise and The Hare: You are walking your own path, in your own time. You are not following anyone else's lead or letting their actions distract you. You have control over your thoughts and actions. You know yourself!

And when you have reached balance in your life, you can feel when your emotions are out of whack, when your feelings are hurt and when you do not feel like yourself. You know there is something bothering you —whether it is hurt from the past or anxiety about the future — that you need to let go of. And when you realize this, you reflect and take the time to address it.

Balance keeps us in sync with ourselves, so as we grow, we can process what needs to stay and what needs to go. Growth and change are inevitable in life, and when you create balance, you can better handle the ups and downs. You flow with the stream of change — and not against it.

Checking and Balancing into the Future

Balance sounds pretty ideal, doesn't it? But the challenge that comes with balance is that once we attain it, it is not a one-time fix. Life happens, children happen, work happens, family happens. When major life events happen, we can be thrown off balance.

But the key to staying steady is grounding your balance in who you are — and you do that with your mantra.

Like I stated earlier, my mantra is, "I will have peace and happiness today and everyday of my life." That means when bad things happen, I continue to be rooted in who I am. I do not panic, I do not start people-pleasing, I don't get negative. I go through the stages of letting go, and in the process, I am constantly guided by my mantra. I handle each situation as it comes and I remain peaceful and happy, continuing to stay aware, to forgive and to remain balanced.

The Art of Letting Go is a daily process that keeps you grounded with what is important to you, who you want to be and what type of life you want to live. And your mantra is one of your greatest tools to stay focused on the process.

Balance of Personal Power

During this process, and especially during the balance stage, you learn to make yourself a priority. That may seem selfish, but I assure you it is not. You have to nourish yourself, so you are able to help others and be the best wife, husband, mom, dad, friend, employee, etc., that you can be. You must see everyday as a chance to move forward, to be patient with yourself (even in your mistakes) and to smile at yourself all the time.

In balance, you are constantly looking at yourself, your thoughts and your actions. In doing this, your are clearly examining your mistakes and becoming aware of what needs to happen so you will not make the same mistakes over and over again. Having balance is like holding up a mirror that honestly examines your whole being, including your emotional and mental state. It allows you to look deeply at yourself and clearly envision your strengths and weaknesses.

Handling the Good With the Bad

As you continue to conquer and overcome and use all of these tools to let go of the old and embrace your future, I think it's valuable to discuss how a balanced perspective changes our view of ourselves, our experiences and the world around us.

In our lives, there are some things we can prepare for, and there are certain stages in life that we know are coming. Of course, there are wonderful experiences that are out of our control. You might say, "What about the negative experiences that happen to us? Are they wonderful?" And my answer: Yes, definitely.

When we experience the hard times in life, they become great opportunities to show what we are made of. Remember, diversity doesn't build character, adversity does. So when a situation knocks you on your butt — and it will — sit there, cry a little and throw a tantrum. Then, you wipe your tears, get up, sink your heels in and remember who you are.

As you work on being balanced and letting go, you will quickly learn that you are not immune to heartbreak, frustration, anger or sadness. But you can become immune to staying stuck and avoiding your challenges. You can now move forward. You have a box of tools that will help you through the hardest of situations and keep you focused on yourself, your goals and your future.

ABOUT THE AUTHOR

Suntia is a Licensed Clinical Social Worker & Couples Therapist who uses proven emotion-focused techniques and cognitive behavioral methodologies to help her clients deal with everyday life and relationship struggles better. By taking a positive, proactive and practical approach to emotional well-being, Suntia teaches others how to develop a stronger sense of self, so they can love deeper and live lighter.

Made in the USA
Lexington, KY
29 January 2017